The Song of
Beowulf

A NEW TRANSCREATION

T0327029

Dedication

This translation is dedicated to the memory of
Davis Taylor (1942–2016),
who read early drafts and advised well.

The Song of
Beowulf

A NEW TRANSCREATION

J.D. WINTER

sussex
ACADEMIC
PRESS
Brighton • Portland • Toronto

2 4 6 8 10 9 7 5 3 1

First published 2018, in Great Britain by
SUSSEX ACADEMIC PRESS
PO Box 139
Eastbourne BN24 9BP

Distributed in North America by
SUSSEX ACADEMIC PRESS
ISBS Publisher Services
920 NE 58th Ave #300, Portland, OR 97213, USA

British Library Cataloguing in Publication Data
A CIP catalogue record for this book is available from the British Library.

Library of Congress Cataloging-in-Publication Data
Applied for.

Typeset & designed by Sussex Academic Press, Brighton & Eastbourne.
Printed by TJ International, Padstow, Cornwall.

Contents

Acknowledgement

I cannot thank enough my tutor in Anglo-Saxon of 1963, Richard Hamer. Approached after all that time he agreed to check the text. Painstakingly and minutely he did so, with an eye for inaccuracy of interpretation and an ear for infelicity of word usage. I have taken his advice in the vast majority of instances; the errors that remain are mine alone.

Introduction

The manuscript of *Beowulf* dates from about 1000 AD but the poem was made or in the making perhaps two centuries earlier. It may have taken shape under a long and varied history of oral performance, undergoing what is known as pre-literary composition in the manner of old epic. Outside reference shows ours was by no means the first manuscript but it is the only one from the time. A fine account of the poem's background, covering manuscript, text, origin, history and legend and much else, is to be found in the excellent Klaeber and Wrenn editions (1922 and 1953), which I have made extensive use of. Chambers' *Introduction to the Study of the Poem* (third edition 1959) has also been of great interest. And I have plagued the internet with question after question, as all can do, and learnt much thereby.

But I have learnt most, naturally enough, from engaging with the text by way of translation. It has yielded up a story at once simpler and deeper than I remembered from my undergraduate days, in a poetic voice that takes the breath away as one hears it. I cannot recommend the reader too warmly to discover at least something of the original. As regards the narrative detail I believe extensive notes are not needed – the story tells itself – and a very light commentary at the start of each section will I hope be signpost enough for the reader. In it I have included one or two thoughts of my own, merely as a possible aid, and not to impose direction. Whatever takes place in the space between poet's and listener's or reader's mind, the impulse is to free and not to steer. A journey is offered: that is all one can say.

To retrace the *Beowulf*-poet's voyage I have rigged up a rather different vessel from that employed by Seamus Heaney in his version of 1999. His makes for an exciting trip. It has the weather of that first crossing between minds, the sun and thunder in the life of a hero, the jubilation and dismay of the people and peoples about him, the near-numinous quality of the places we come to and pass by, the hall of Heorot, the monsters' lake, the dragon's hoard. It is a great read and unlikely to be superseded. But there is always room for a new approach: and mine is to do with the poetic voice. The extraordinary sinew of the verse in the original, the brilliance and force of its compressed economy and alliterative power, is beyond the reach of modern English. Ezra Pound in his *Seafarer* conveys a hint of what Anglo-Saxon verse is capable of, but a century later such an archaistic mode as his – and there is no other way to do what he did – is unacceptable. William Gummere's is a *Beowulf* of Pound's time, ornate in a different way, also reliant on an outdated vocabulary and syntax. My approach depends on a simple question: in the translation of a poem, whose pulse is it that beats through the words?

I have tried to be faithful to the original heart-beat. My whole endeavour has been to let it come through, in however faint an echo. I have kept the vocabulary simple, retained something of the literal power of a number of the kennings (metaphorical expressions such as 'world's candle' for 'sun'), shown the sections of the poem as in the manuscript, and added a visible caesura to the lines. The vocabulary in my view needs to reflect a steady register, that can be readily associated with the world it speaks of. The kennings are a poetic delight. The sections, marked by Roman numerals in the original as here, in several cases are complete and powerful episodes in themselves. The visible caesura, present in printed editions of the original though not in the manuscript, I think is useful in allowing the pace of the poem not to become too hurried. The Anglo-Saxon poetic line of two alliterated halves, with highly-charged compressed phrases often employing compound words, offers the mind a good deal to absorb within a given space. The convention of printing it with a gap at the caesura makes the reading easier and leaves the time needed for poetic niceties and weight of meaning to sink in; and I have adopted the convention in my presentation here. There is a gradualness to the original, I feel: it cannot be rushed. The manuscript gives no space to line-breaks or to line-endings; but the spoken poem must always have made good use of pause. There is too much at stake for it to be otherwise. In line with the printed Anglo-Saxon, then, and with what I sense to be the current of the original, I offer a lay-out that gives the alliteration a moment to make its effect; and for the cargo as a whole to be taken on board.

Without aspiring to the assonant power of the original, I have let the modern language discover an alliterative binding in each line, to underpin the two halves and to offer an echo of the distant forge of the past. Sometimes I let the start of a syllable stand in for the start of a word; sometimes I allow a minor word or words to sound out the pattern. But for the most part what is on offer here has more of a direct suggestion of the original, if with nothing like its force. Alliterative power is less now than it was. The failing is as much of the modern language as of the modern writer. Before rhyme came to be adopted in Western poetry the poetic construct drew more, far more, on its light hammer-blows, an initial force driving on the whole; and yet nothing is harsh. The original text of *Beowulf* has a finish to it that allows it, as a great work of art, to rest easy on the mind, as the adventure takes one on and forward.

One may even sense in *Beowulf* the poetry of a sea-faring nation, the light movement of the waters touching the line. The nation is not England or Sweden or Denmark. It is an intermin-gled part of Northern Europe using the West Saxon dialect of the language in England to convey a mix of Scandinavian history and Teutonic legend; and to realise a portrait, through story, of the universal human. It is a timely reminder of the mixture of races and influences in every country. As far as the lexical meaning is concerned, it is all in the pages that follow, if not always in quite the same order as in each original sentence and phrase. But there is a song, that I have done no more than catch at, at the heart. Beyond my or any transcreation it remains, calling out to be re-discovered.

JDW 2018

The Song of
Beowulf

The poem begins with an introduction to the kingly line of the land where the hero's first exploits are to take place. Danes often take a prefix: Spear-Danes, East-Danes, Ring-Danes. Scyld Scefing is the first of the current dynasty; the account of the solemnities at his passing has a tone of something of later significance: transience perhaps. The text twice mentions his son as Beowulf, which seems to be a scribal error for Beow.

Listen! Of a high   royal line we hear tell,   1–52
the glory of Spear-Danes   in days gone by,
princely warriors   and powerful deeds!
   Often Scyld Scefing   faced the enemy;
from many a tribe   the hall and mead-benches
he seized, to spread terror.   In early times
he was found helpless.   But he took heart,
got strong on the earth   and strove in honour,
till there were none   of the near-settlers
over the whale-road   that were not ruled;
but all gave tribute.   A true king was he!
Later a boy   was born at court:
God had sent   an infant son
as a help to the people.   He had seen the hardship
and crime in the land   when it was leaderless
for a long time.   The Lord of Life
and Guardian of Glory   gave mortal honour
to Beow, Scyld's boy –   broad was his fame,
far-distant and near,   in the land of the Danes.
So should a young man   mean to do good
by generous gifts   in his father's guidance,
so that in old age   or event of war,
friendly companions   still stand firm,
true to their lord.   In every tribe
a man shall do well   by deeds of worth.
   Then at the strict hour   Scyld, very strong,
left for the path   of the Lord's protection.

They took him out   to the ocean's tide
as he had directed   his dear companions,
when the prince of the Danes   had the power of words,
a beloved leader   who long held sway.
There a ring-prow   rested at harbour,
the king's ship, ice-covered,   eager to go.
They laid him down,   their cherished leader,
sharer of treasures,   in the ship's lap,
famous by the mast.   Many ornaments,
a great wealth was gathered,   got from afar.
No boat have I heard of   that looked so handsome:
weapons of war,   warriors' clothing,
breastplates, swords,   a bright stack of treasures
in its lap laden   lay with him there,
to go far out   in the power of the flood.
The gifts they gave,   great valuables,
were no less grand   than the gifts given
by those who had launched him   alone on the ocean
in the beginning   as a young boy.
Over his head   now they set high
a golden banner   and let the waves bear him,
gave him to the sea.   They were sad at heart,
mournful in mind.   Men do not know,
counsellors in hall,   heroes under heaven,
none truly can tell   who took in that cargo.

I

The feud between son-in-law and father-in-law that led to the destruction of Heorot by fire is a legendary event that falls outside the poem's time-scale but that its audience would have known of. It is alluded to later by Beowulf, as if in anticipatory foreboding, in a speech at his homecoming. Onela also comes up towards the end of the story: in a separate family feud he is to plague the royal house of Beowulf's land.

Grendel's introduction, set in austerely Christian terms, adds a trace of a homiletic element that appears here and there in the poem, but that in no way dispels the atmosphere of heroic legend.

Then in the strongholds   for a long stretch   53–114
Beow of the Danes,   beloved king,
was famed in the tribes;   his father had gone,
the leader from the land.   At length a son,
Healfdene, was born.   A battle-grim hero,
in age he led   the land with glory.
To the chief of hosts   were four children born:
one after another   woke into the world,
Heorogar and Hrothgar,   Halga the good;
and one, I heard,   was Onela's queen,
neck-close bed-fellow   to the war-king of the Swedes.
   Now to Hrothgar   was high renown granted,
good fortune in war,   so that his followers
yearned to obey him,   till the young warriors
made a great band.   A spacious building
it entered his mind   to order up,
to have a mighty   mead-hall made,
more majestic   than the sons of men
had ever heard tell.   Here he would hand on
to young and to old   all that God yielded him,
except public land   and the lives of people.
And I heard of a task   laid upon tribes
here and there   throughout this world,
the hall's adornment.   All in due time
it came to pass   that it was prepared,
a wondrous place.   And he whose word
was heard far and wide   named it Heorot.
So Hrothgar held true   and handed out rings,
treasure at the table.   The hall towered high,
wide-gabled, awaiting   the thrust of war

9

and enemy flame.   Not yet was a feud
of bitter strife born   between son-in-law
and father-in-law,   by a foul deed fostered.
   A powerful demon   that dwelt in darkness
heard in anguish   every day
the rising sound   of the roar of revel
high in the hall,   the note of the harp,
the clear cry of the singer.   He sang, who knew
the old account   of the origin of men,
how the Almighty   made the Earth,
the water-locked land   that is lovely to look at.
The Victory-Strong   set the sun and the moon
as a great light   to gleam on groundlings,
adorning the land   with an array
of tree-limb and leaf;   and he shaped life
for every kind   of moving creature.
So the liegemen   lived in delight,
fine and free,   until a hell-fiend
undertook   an act of evil.
Grendel was   the grim being's name,
famed in the borders;   the moor and fen,
the wasteland was his.   The luckless one
had been confined   with the kin of monsters,
after the Creator   had condemned them
when he took revenge   on the race of Cain,
the eternal Lord,   for the onslaught on Abel.
He frowned on the feud,   and for the offence
he drove the murderer   far from mankind.
From Cain sprang   all monstrous offspring,
ogres and elves   and evil shades
of the dead, and giants   who jostled with God
a weary age.   He paid them well for it.

II

The poet describes Grendel's first incursion and regrets the unavailing state of the pre-Christian community from which the victims were drawn.

When night had come   the creature came near   115–188
to see how the Ring-Danes   took their rest
after beer-time   in the tall building.
Fast asleep   after the feasting
he saw the nobles;   they knew not sorrow,
misery of men.   In a moment ready,
the cruel and malign   creature of damnation
in a savage greed   grabbed thirty men
from where they slept,   to slouch off home
exulting in plunder,   padding the path
back to his dwelling   with his fill of death.
    Then at dawn,   at day's beginning,
men soon learnt   of Grendel's might.
So the feast   was followed by weeping,
loud morning-lament.   The illustrious king,
ruler most royal,   wretchedly sat,
the mighty one   in grief for his men.
All had seen   the enemy spoor
of the cursed demon.   Too foul was that carnage,
loathsome and lasting.   It took no longer
than one night more   for still more murders.
Nor did the cruel one   rue his killing,
his violent sin.   He was too set on it.
Now easy to find   was the man who elsewhere
kept his bed   in the out-buildings,
once he had learnt   how things lay,
and taken to heart   the envious hatred
of the hall's new ruler.   They hid themselves
further off, safer,   far from the fiend.

One against all,   opposed to the right,
he lorded it,   till silent lay
the best of buildings.   Long was it borne:
the king of the Danes   darkly endured
for twelve winters' space   woe upon woe,
his fill of sorrows.   So it gained fame
with the sons of men,   as the story spread
sadly in songs,   how Grendel strove
an age with Hrothgar.   Such hatred he bore,
malign and vicious   for many half-years,
always at war.   He wished not for peace
with any Dane.   His deadly evil
he would not abate,   nor offer blood-payment –
no counsellor need   seek compensation,
shining coin   at the hands of the slayer!
Still the demon,   the dark shade of death,
went in search   of young warriors and old,
hovering and plotting.   In thick night he held
the misty moors.   Men do not know
where those of hell's craft   creep out on their way.
    A mass of evil   was all his making,
the fatal lone-goer   and foe of mankind,
a heap of harm.   At Heorot he stayed
in the dark nights,   the rich-decked hall;
but up to the gift-seat   he dared not go,
in holy fear,   and far from all love.
    In deep distress   the king of the Danes
grieved at heart.   Men of high counsel
often sat   in search of a plan
for the best way   for bold-minded warriors
to attack this source   of sudden terror.
Sometimes they promised   at their prayer-places
honour to idols,   earnestly asking
the demon-slayer   to deliver the people

in their hard need.   Such was their habit,
their heathen custom,   calling to mind
hellish thoughts,   unaware of the High One,
the Judge of Deeds,   distant from the Lord.
Not at all could they praise   Heaven's Protector,
the Ruler of Glory.   Wretched be the man
who thrown into hardship   shall thrust his soul
to the fire's embrace: he shall find no comfort,
nor one whit change!   Good cheer be his
who seeks to discover   the Lord after death's day,
so to find peace   in the Father's arms!

III

*Géats (also Weders): Beowulf's tribe in the south of Sweden. The
Danish coastguard's speech is the first of many exchanges of courtesy and
correctness between peoples.*

Healfdene's son   seethed in anguish   189–257
at the time's woe.   Nor could the wise one
lay down his grief: the carnage was too grim,
direst in cruelty,   darkest of night-crimes,
loathsome and lasting,   that fell on his landfolk.
    A famed warrior,   a follower of Hygelac,
heard from afar   in his Géat homeland
of Grendel's acts.   In all the world
in sheer strength then   he was outstanding,
a mighty noble.   He bid be made
a strong wave-goer;   and swore to seek
across the swan's way   the warlike king
of honoured name   who had need of men.
Wise men cherished him,   yet they chided him
not at all   for the adventure,
but championed him,   checking the omens.

13

From the Géat tribe   the great-heart took
a chosen band,   the bravest of all
that he could find.   Fifteen men
made for the woodenboat.   The warrior leader,
skilled at sea-craft,   showed them the coast-lines.
   Time went by.   On the wave the boat waited
under the cliff.   Keen to be off
they stepped onto the prow.   The tide-streams turned,
sea against sand.   To the ship's lap
fine armour was borne,   bright ornaments.
So they shoved out   the well-framed ship,
the warriors, restless   to be on their way.
Then it went like a bird   on the billowy sea,
the foamy-necked boat,   flung on far
by the wind, till it came,   the curved-prow, to where,
after due time   on the next day
the travellers all   looked out on land,
ocean-cliffs shining,   the sheer headlands,
broad capes of the sea.   The crossing was done,
the wave-going over.   The Weder troop
quickly stepped out   onto the shore,
mooring the woodenboat.   Their mail rattled,
their garments of war;   and they thanked God
the ocean-voyage   was easily done.
   The Danish watchman   whose duty it was
to guard the sea-cliff   saw from the height
bright bucklers and armour,   battle-ready, borne
across the gangway.   His interest grew
as he wondered   who the men were.
Hrothgar's follower   rode on horseback
down to the shore,   mightily shook
his strongwood spear,   and stiffly spoke:
   "Who are you   in all your armour,
corslet-clad,   coming by water,

sailing this   tall ship of yours
over the sea-road?   For a long space
I have kept watch   as coast-guard here,
in case an enemy   with a ship-army
brings danger to   the Danish land.
None ever arrived   more openly
with linden shields;   yet the right to land,
the royal word   from the warlike kinsmen,
has not been sent.   I have not seen on Earth
as mighty a man   as that armed warrior
in this force of yours.   If his form does not lie,
his matchless appearance,   he is no mere hall-man
ennobled with weapons.   Now I must know,
before you go forward   and further on
as lying spies   in the land of the Danes –
of what race are you?   Now you sea-rovers
far from home,   it is best to make haste.
You must understand   my mind's intent,
and clearly say   from where you are come."

IV

Beowulf's first words tell of his background and indicate leadership.
The poem is as much about his character as his deeds. The human and
responsible figure of the coastguard is one of a number of minor characters
that stay in the mind.

The leader then   unlocked his word-store,   258–319
the eldest of them,   answering him:
"Of Géat blood   are we men born,
hearth-companions   of Hygelac.
Famed in the tribes   was my father;
he was Ecgtheow,   an acclaimed general.
Many winters were his   till his way took him on,

the old one from home.   Far and wide on the earth
every wise man   remembers him well.
We have come here   with friendship at heart
to seek your sovereign,   Healfdene's son,
the people's guardian: give us good counsel!
Our errand is   an urgent one
to the famous lord.   There is a matter —
no secret, I think.   You know, if it is
as we in truth   have heard it told:
among the Danes   dwells some strange enemy
of hateful deed,   who in dark of night
leaves a hellish   heap of carnage,
unheard-of foulness.   I can unfold
a plan to Hrothgar   with open heart,
how in wisdom and worth   he can worst the foe,
if he is ever   to see a reversal,
and seek relief   from his suffering.
And so the surge   of sorrow will cool,
or else his ill fortune   will never be over,
the burden he bears,   for as long as the best
of buildings stays   in its high station."

   The watchman spoke,   where he sat on his horse,
the fearless officer.   "One from the other,
words and actions,   an able warrior
with a keen wit   can tell apart.
This troop is friendly,   as I find it,
to the king of the Danes.   Continue your way
with weapons and armour;   I will guide you.
And I will call on   my young company
to guard with honour,   against all enemies,
your newly-tarred   sea-traveller,
the ship on the sand,   till on the deep stream
the boat with twisted   neck takes back
a beloved one   to the Géat border.

To such a good man   be it given
to see out safe   the storm of battle."
    They went on their way.   The wide-decked boat
rode on its hawser,   staying at rest,
fast at anchor.   Above the helmets
the boar-crests glittered,   adorned with gold,
fire-hardened, glinting,   each guarding a life.
They marched off together,   men quick to the fray,
hurrying on   till the well-timbered hall,
gold-stained and splendid,   lay in their sight,
the most famous building   beneath the skies
for dwellers on earth,   the abode of the king.
The land was lit   far and wide by its light.
The warlike protector   pointed it out,
the gleaming hall,   the home of heroes,
for them to make haste to.   Wheeling his horse,
the worthy warrior   said these words:
"It is time for me to go.   May the Almighty
in his kindness   keep you safe
for the great deed!   I will depart
to stay on guard   against invaders."

V

The formalities continue. Wulfgar the Vandal (probably from Vendel in Uppland, Sweden) may be serving the Danish king in gratitude for refuge as an exile; or simply as an adventurous traveller. There is a certain amount in the story's background that its contemporary audience would have been familiar with, but that to us is a matter of guesswork, or mere mystery.

Paved with stone   was the street that led   320–370
the close group of men.   War-corslets glittered;
the hard iron ringlets,   hand-linked and shining,

sang in the armour.   In fearful array
at once to the hall   they hastened along;
till weary from the sea   they set down their shields,
broad, wondrous hard,   at the building's wall,
and bent to the bench   with breastplates ringing,
the gear of battle.   All together
stood the spears,   the grey ashwood shafts
of an iron-clad troop   of travellers by sea
of high note in its arms.   A proud noble there
asked the warriors   of their ancestry.

"From where do you hail   in your mask-helmets,
your grey shirts of mail   and gold-plated shields,
your horde of war-shafts?   I am Hrothgar's
liegeman and messenger.   I never saw so many
men from afar   as fearless as you.
I think as true heroes,   in greatness of heart
you come to seek Hrothgar,   not exiles in hardship."
Renowned for his fighting,   fierce under his helmet,
the Géat leader   gave his reply
in a few words.   "We are Hygelac's
board-companions.   Beowulf is my name.
I wish to speak   with Healfdene's son,
the famous leader   and your lord,
of my errand,   if it accords
that we may meet   so noble a man."
Wulfgar replied,   the Vandal prince –
the man's shrewdness   was known to many,
as well as his valour –   "I will advise
the Danish king   as you desire,
the noble ruler   of your request,
Scyld's great-grandson,   giver of treasure –
and soon inform you   of his answer,
the famous one,   as he thinks fit."
    He turned and hurried   to where Hrothgar sat

old and grey   in a group of his nobles.
Warlike, he strode   to stand at the shoulder
of the Danish king;   he knew courtly custom.
Wulfgar spoke   to his dear sovereign:
   "Géat tribesmen   have travelled here
over the sea's track   from afar;
the band's captain   is called Beowulf
by his men of war.   If it be your will,
my lord, these warriors   wish with you
an exchange of words.   Allow it so,
gracious Hrothgar,   and grant them answer.
In their war-gear   they seem worth
the respect of men.   To my mind the leader,
who brought them here,   is one of high bearing."

VI

*Hrethel is the father of Hygelac, the present king of the Géats. (He is
also Beowulf's grandfather.) His passing in sorrow at the death of
another of his sons is described in XXXIV, XXXV. The sombre tone
Beowulf ends on here is a counterpoise to the Danish king's excitement.
He refers to the likely absence of a body to bury, if he loses. (A corpse's
head was covered for burial both in ancient Scandinavia and among the
Anglo-Saxons.)*

Hrothgar spoke,   helm of the Danes: 371–455
"I knew him   in his boyhood.
Ecgtheow was   his old father's name;
Hrethel of the Géats   gave his one daughter
to him for his home.   Their hardy son now
has travelled here   to find a true friend.
It has been said   by certain sailors,
who took gifts of treasure   there for the Géats
as a sign of regard,   that this renowned warrior

has the sheer might   of thirty men
in his hand-grip.   Holy God
in his high kindness   has sent him here
to us the Danes,   I do not doubt it,
against Grendel's terror.   I shall grant gifts
to the good man   for his great courage.
Be quick and tell   the brotherly band
to come and attend us   all together;
make it clear in words   that they are welcome
to the Danish race!"   To the hall door
went Wulfgar to speak   to the men waiting:
"My victorious lord,   leader of the Danes,
says that he knows   of your noble background;
and you who are all   heroes at heart
are welcome here   across the sea-waves.
Now you may go   in your mask-helmets
and all your war-gear   to greet Hrothgar.
But let your shields and spears,   deadly shafts,
here await   the issue of words."
    The mighty man rose,   and more about him,
a splendid band;   some stayed behind
to guard the weapons   as he gave word.
Led by their guide   the group went quickly
under Heorot's roof.   The war-hardened one strode,
stern under his helmet,   till he stood in the hall.
Beowulf spoke –   his breastplate shone,
the armour-net linked   by the art of the smith –
    "Greetings, Hrothgar!   I am Hygelac's
kinsman and warrior.   Many deeds of worth
were mine in my youth.   Of this matter of Grendel
I have heard tell   at home in my land.
Seafarers say   that this fair building,
this unmatched hall   lies empty and useless
to every man   when the evening sun

hides below   the clear face of heaven.
I was persuaded   by my people,
the best of men   and the most wise,
prince Hrothgar,   to approach you here.
They understand   the extent of my strength;
they found out   when I was back from the fray,
blood-stained from the enemy.   I had bound five,
blighted a monstrous brood,   rained blows by night
on water-demons.   Much I endured
to avenge the Weders   and ravage their enemies.
They brought grief on themselves.   As for Grendel,
I would accomplish   an outcome alone
against the dread monster.   And so I desire,
prince of the Bright-Danes,   powerful protector
of the race of Scyld,   to make a request.
Defender of warriors,   dear king of the people,
do not refuse me,   I have come so far.
Let me and my band,   these battle-hard men,
with no other help   bring health to Heorot.
And since I hear   the hellish thing
pays in its pride   no heed to weapons,
I scorn at heart –   and so may Hygelac,
my own liege lord,   look kindly on me –
to carry a sword   or a broad shield,
a yellow buckler.   In mortal battle
I shall grasp the enemy   in my hand's grip,
foe against foe.   In the Lord's guidance
let him trust   whom death takes hold of.
I expect him to come   to the hall when he can,
eager to slay,   to devour at his ease
great men of battle –   my Géat troops –
as often before.   There is no bound duty
to cover my corpse-head.   Blood-becluttered
let him clutch me,   if death claim me.

He will take the gory   body to taste it,
the lone marauder,   and ruthlessly rend it,
blood-marking the moor.   Put out of your mind
further care   for my fit disposal.
If I am struck down,   send to Hygelac
the best of battle-garments,   finest of breastplates,
my body's protector.   Hrethel bequeathed it;
it was Weland's work.   Fate goes as it will!"

VII

*There is a suggestion of a debt to Hrothgar on the part of Beowulf's
family. But it is in no way claimed. It happens, too, that Hrothgar's
wife Wealhtheow is descended from a Wylfing king. There is an
inevitable backcloth of a certain tribal interweaving. While debts of
honour are important in the story, in this case Beowulf's offer is freely
made and freely accepted.*

*In the past there has been feuding between the Danes and the Géats
(referred to fleetingly in XXVI); the sense of festive unity at the end
here may be a little heightened thereby.*

Hrothgar spoke,   helm of the Danes: 456–498
"Out of kindness   you have come to us,
Beowulf my friend,   to fight for our cause.
Your father started   a deep-felt feud
when he slew by hand   Heatholaf
of the Wylfing tribe.   In fear of war
the Weders could not   keep him with them.
And so he sought   Scyld's honoured line,
the people of the Danes   past the rolling wave.
Then first I led   the Danish folk:
I ruled in my youth   a glorious realm,
a rich home for heroes.   Heoregar had died,
my elder brother   alive no more,

Healfdene's son: he was better than I!
Later I finished   the feud with money.
I sent to the Wylfings   over the water's back
ancient treasures.   He swore oaths to me.
To mention the present   matter at all
grieves my heart,   the hurt that Grendel
racks me with,   his deeds of wrath,
his raids on Heorot.   My hall-troop is thinned;
fate swept them off   to the fearsome monster.
Yet the power of God   may easily part
the rash destroyer   from his deeds!
Over the ale-cup   again and again,
drunk with beer,   my men boasted
that in the ale-hall   they would await
Grendel's attack   with the grim sword.
Then in the morning   this mead-building
in day's gleam   was stained with gore,
the bench-planks all   made wet with blood,
carnage in the hall.   My company is smaller,
my dear trusty band,   since death took them off.
Sit now at the feast,   and as you think fit,
give us a hero's   tale from the heart!"
    Then for the Géat-men   all together
in the beer-hall   a bench was cleared;
there the stout-hearted   went and sat,
proud in their strength.   A servant who bore
the adorned ale-cup   looked after the serving
of the shining sweet drink.   At times a singer
sang clearly in Heorot.   There was revelry of heroes,
a great warrior band,   the Danes and the Weders.

VIII

Unferth is a colourful character whom we meet later in somewhat more laudable circumstances. The epic swimming contest of Beowulf's youth, that turns into a story of survival, seems to herald a part of the forthcoming story.

Unferth spoke, Ecglaf's son, 499–558
who sat at the Danish sovereign's foot.
Greatly vexed at the adventure of Beowulf,
the valiant seafarer, he gave vent to his thoughts:
for he did not admit that another man
on earth had ever accomplished more deeds
of high rank and glory than himself.
"Are you the Beowulf who vied with Breca
and strove in swimming on the wide sea,
where you two proudly tried the waters,
and for a vain boast ventured your lives
upon the deep? None could deter you
from the folly, not friend nor foe,
when you two went swimming upon the waves.
There you each embraced the current,
measured the sea-paths, with swift-moving arms
cut through the waters. The waves swirled up
in wintry surges; in the stream's power
seven nights you swept on; and he outswam you,
he had more strength. Then in the morning
the sea took him up to the Réam tribe's shore.
He made his way, a man loved by his people,
back to his home, the land of the Brondings,
to the fair stronghold where he held sway,
his castle and treasure. In truth he made good
all that he swore, the son of Béanstan.
And so I expect a worse issue for you –
though you prevail here and there in the press

and drive of battle –   if you dare await
Grendel night-long   at a time near at hand."
   The son of Ecgtheow,   Beowulf, spoke:
"More than enough,   my friend Unferth,
drunk with beer,   you've dwelt on Breca,
retold his trials!   But I count it the truth
that I had more strength   in the wave-struggle.
More sea-might was mine   than any man.
When we were boys   both of us
made a bond,   still being young;
and we two swore   that out in the sea
we'd hazard our lives: and we held to that.
Each with a bare sword   boldly in hand
we swam in the sea,   intent to save
ourselves from whales;   not a whit could he swim
away from me,   far into flood-waves,
faster in water;   nor would I forsake him.
We two stayed   in the sea together
for a space of five nights,   till the flood split us up,
the surging sea,   the coldest of storms
in the darkening night,   as a north wind,
war-fierce, attacked us.   Rough were the waves,
and the minds of sea-fish   were stirred against us.
There against enemies   I was aided
by my mail-shirt,   hand-linked and mighty,
the battle-garment   locked on my breast,
adorned with gold.   A deadly ravager
seized me and dragged me   down to the sea-bed
in its awful grip;   still I was granted
with my sword's   sharp edge of war
to trouble the monster.   So my hand trounced
the mighty sea-beast   in the rush of battle.

IX

Beowulf's reply to Unferth does not avoid a telling aside (that appears acceptable in context) on the Danish defensive shortcomings. Hrothgar's and Wealhtheow's words of welcome, at once regal and warm, conclude the formalities before the first main encounter.

"Hard and often,   hateful evil-doers   559–661
set about me: I did them service
as was fitting   with my fearsome sword.
The foul things had   no joy of the feast,
of tasting me,   those terrible creatures,
swarming to a banquet   at the sea-bottom;
but in the morning,   maimed and slain,
they lay up   along the sea-wrack,
sent to sleep   by the sword, no more
to harass journeyers   on the high seas
in their crossing.   Light came from the east,
God's bright beacon;   the waters abated;
I set my eyes   upon sea-headlands,
wind-swept cliffs.   Fate often saves
an undoomed man   if he dare all.
It was my fortune   to fell with the sword
nine water-demons.   I have heard no word
under heaven's vault   of a harder night's fighting,
a man more oppressed   in the ocean's currents.
So I escaped   the clutches of enemies,
weary as I was.   The waves bore me on,
the surging waters   of the sea-current,
to the land of the Lapps.   Not in the least
have I heard tell   of such dire terror
from your sword.   Such savage blows
at battle-play –   I do not boast –
never did Breca's   blood-stained blade
once achieve.   Nor yours either,

26

though you became   your brothers' killer,
your nearest kinsmen.   For that you will know
damnation in hell,   despite your quick tongue.
I say to you truly,   son of Ecglaf,
never would Grendel,   that grim monster,
have wrought such outrage   against your ruler,
such horror in Heorot,   if your heart and mind
were as fierce for combat   as you yourself claim.
But he has found out   he need not fear
the assault overmuch   of your own people,
the dread sword-storm   of the Victory-Danes.
He takes his toll,   extending no mercy
to the Danish people,   but slays, sends to death
at will – with not much   of a hostile welcome
at the Spear-Danes' hands!   But very soon
I shall show him a fight,   the force and the strength
of the Géat race.   Then go he who may
brave to the mead-hall,   when morning's light,
the gaily-dressed sun   of another day,
shines from the south   on the sons of men!"
   The grey war-hero,   the giver of treasure
was light at heart;   the lord of the Bright-Danes
was sure of his aid.   The shepherd of the people
had found in Beowulf   a firm intention.
There was laughter of heroes,   heartiest sound,
fair words were spoken.   Wealhtheow went forward
as was the custom,   Hrothgar's queen,
decked in gold,   to greet the warriors,
graciously handing   the brimming goblet
first to the Danish   land's defender.
She wished the beloved   leader joy
at the taking of mead.   With a will he tasted
the cup and the feast,   the war-famed king.
Then she went round   to old warriors and young,

the descendant of Helm,   all over the hall
with the costly cup,   till the moment came
that the spirited queen,   splendid with rings,
carried to Beowulf   the beaker of mead.
She greeted the Géats,   giving God thanks,
wise in her words,   that her wish had been granted –
that in one man   she might set her trust
to combat the evil.   Accepting the cup
from Wealhtheow's hands,   the war-hardened warrior
made a pledge of faith,   ready for the fray.
The son of Ecgtheow,   Beowulf, said:
"When I embarked   and sat in the sea-boat
with my warrior band,   it was my wish
that I should work   your people's will
to the full, or if not,   fall in battle
in the foe's dread grasp.   A deed I shall do,
an exploit of worth,   or my day-of-ending
I shall meet   in the mead-hall here."
The lady was pleased   at the proud promise
of the Géat's words.   Gold-decked, she turned,
the land's noble queen,   to sit next to her lord.
   Then again as before   the people were glad
in the hall, and words   of high honour were spoken;
the revel of victory   rose up. Soon
Healfdene's son   desired to seek
his nightly rest.   He knew the monster
plotted a raid   on the royal hall
when the sun's light   could be seen no longer
and night's gloom   gathered all over,
and shapes came striding,   shrouded in dark,
black under the clouds.   The company rose.
One man approached   the other then,
Hrothgar bid Beowulf   the best of fortune,
handing the wine-hall   into his care:

"To no-one before   but only you,
since my hand   first hefted a shield,
have I entrusted   the Danes' great hall.
Have now and hold   the best of houses:
be brave, be strong,   be mindful of glory,
keep watch for the foe!   All you wish is yours
if you survive   this feat of valour."

X

*References to the Lord's overarching power are finely balanced with those
to Beowulf's own and finite strength. Throughout the poem there is the
sense of a dominantly Christian god, if one may put it like that, under-
lying a stage set for deeds of epic prowess.*

Then Hrothgar left   with his band of heroes,   662–709
the Scyldings' defender   departed the hall;
the war-chief wished   to seek out Wealhtheow,
his queen and bedfellow.   It went about
that the Sovereign of Glory   had sent a hall-guard
against the monster;   that a man had been found
by the king of the Danes   to counter Grendel.
In truth the warrior   had a deep trust
both in his own force   and in the Lord's favour.
Then he cast off   his iron corslet
and helmet, handing   his adorned sword,
the best of blades,   to an armour-bearer,
and bid him guard   the battle-gear.
Some words he pronounced   of proud intent,
Beowulf of the Géats,   before taking his bed:
"As Grendel counts himself   great in the challenge
of combat, myself   I account no less.
Therefore I shall not   slay him by sword
and so waste his life,   though I could well.

He has no splendid   weapon to strike with
and pierce my shield,   though his power is awesome
in deeds of death.   We two after dark
will do without swords,   if he dare face me
in unarmed combat.   Then to the cause
the holy Lord   allows to be true,
so will he give glory,   God most wise."
The brave warrior lay down;   the cheek-bolster bore
the face of the man.   Around him many
hardy seafarers   lay on their hall-beds.
None of them thought   that they would ever
arrive again   at their own dear dwelling,
their people, the fair home   that fed them when young.
They had heard tell   death's terrible hand
had earlier taken   too many Danes
inside the wine-hall.   But to the Weders
the Lord vouchsafed   victory's weaving,
his aid and support;   and so the enemy
was overcome   through the art of one man,
one person's strength.   It is a plain truth
that mighty God   has power and guidance
over all men.   When in night's murk he came,
the shadow-goer stalking,   the warriors slept
who were to guard   the gabled building,
all but one.   Men well knew
the demon enemy   could not drag them
to the darkness below,   if the Lord did not will it.
But the one awake   who watched for the foe
in fury awaited   the issue of battle.

XI

The noble hall of Heorot has a presence in the story not unlike that of a character itself. "Bone-adorned" may mean it was decorated with antlers.

Under night's mantle   from the moor   710–790
Grendel approached   with God's anger on him.
The evil one meant   to entrap a member
of the human race   in the high hall.
He prowled below   the sky to a place
to gaze at the princely   wine-hall that gleamed
with plated gold.   Before he had passed
the same way, heading   to Hrothgar's home;
but never in his life,   earlier or later,
did he find harder fortune   at a hall-man's hands.
The roaming creature   came up to the building,
a benighted being.   The door, braced firm
in its fired bands,   fell back to his touch.
Angry, with wicked   intent, he swung wide
the building's mouth.   The foe moved quickly
on the patterned floor,   stepping fast forward
with a furious passion.   From his eyes flickered
a ghastly light   that was like a flame.
He saw in the hall   some warriors sleeping,
a troop from one clan   all together,
a heap of young men.   And he laughed in his mind:
the terrible monster   meant to wrest,
before light came,   the life from the body
of each single one.   He savoured the prospect
of a full feast.   But following that night,
it was not his fate   any further to feed
on the race of man.   The mighty one noticed,
Hygelac's kinsman,   how the creature
of evil was set   for a swift assault.

31

The monster was in   no mind to hold back;
he struck out and seized   a sleeping man,
a warrior at rest,   tore him resistlessly,
bit at the bone-lockers,   drank the veins' blood,
swallowed huge chunks,   and soon had devoured
every bit   of the lifeless body,
the hands, the feet.   Then he stepped forward
to make a grab   at the great-hearted hero
on his bed. The demon's   hand bore down
with cruel intent.   At once the man countered,
sitting up in attack   to meet the arm.
The warden of wickedness   soon was aware
he had not met   a mightier hand-grip
in any area   of the earth
in any man.   Deep in his mind
he took fright, but still   none the sooner came free.
His heart longed to leave there,   to flee into hiding,
to the pack of devils;   his plight was like nothing
he ever had met   in his mortal life.
The noble kinsman   of Hygelac recalled
his speech of the evening;   and standing upright,
took full hold, and burst   the other's fingers.
The monster was escaping,   the man closed in;
the infamous creature   craved to flee further
and make his way out   wherever he might,
far off to the fens;   but his finger-might was crushed,
he knew, in that grip.   A grievous journey
the harmful one   had made to Heorot.
The noble hall dinned: on every Dane
fell terror, on each   of the troop's fierce warriors
in the great fortress.   Both fighters were angry,
cruel keepers of the hall.   The room clashed and clanged;
it was a wonder   that the wine-hall
withstood the wild battlers,   that the fair building

did not fall to the ground.　But it was firm-braced
inside and out　by iron bands
of a skilled smith's making.　There many a mead-bench
set heavy with gold,　I have heard it said,
flew up from the floor　as the foes fought.
Wise men of the Scyldings　had earlier supposed
in no person lay　the power or the cunning
to break up the noble　bone-adorned hall,
bring it to fragments,　unless the fire's arms
swallowed it in flame.　A sound rose up
strange and often.　An awful fear
laid hold of all　the North-Danes listening
outside the walls　to a grievous wailing,
God's foe singing　a song of terror,
the cry of the conquered,　the captive of hell
lamenting his pain.　He pinned him tightly,
who had more strength　than any man
alive at that time　on this earth.

XII

The first of three heroic deeds is done.

The defender of men　meant above all　　　791–836
not to let go　the death-carrier alive –
the days of that creature　he counted as worthless
to anyone at all.　One after another
his warriors drew　their ancestral weapons,
longing to protect　the life of their lord,
the far-famed man,　however they might.
But none of Beowulf's　men there knew,
as firm of heart　they entered the fray,
seeking to slice　the foe from all sides
and banish his being –　that of fine blades

over the earth, none might approach
the creature of sin, no sword of combat.
He had worked a spell on weapons of war,
on each iron edge. His end of existence
at that time on this earth
was an awful one. The alien spirit
was to pass far into the power of fiends.
He who before with bloodthirsty heart
had wrought many crimes upon mankind,
feuding with God, at the last found
his bodily frame afforded no aid;
but the courageous kinsman of Hygelac
had him in his hold. Each was hateful,
while he lived, to the other. Anguished in body
was the vile monster; wide open to view
was a great shoulder-wound. The sinews sprang apart,
the bone-lockers burst. Beowulf was granted
glory in battle. Grendel was forced
to flee, weak to death, below the fen-slopes,
to seek a drear dwelling. The count of his days,
the end of his life was at last upon him –
he knew it well. The wish of all Danes
after the battle-storm came to be.

  Now he had cleansed Hrothgar's hall;
the wise and fierce-hearted warrior from afar
had won it from woe. He revelled in the night-work,
the deed of glory. The Géat men's leader
had kept his proud promise to the Danish people.
All the suffering, the malice-sprung sorrow,
now it was lifted, all they had lived through,
in dire compulsion been made to endure,
no small source of grief. A strong sign it was
when the war-hardy one hung up the hand,
the arm and the shoulder – there all together
was Grendel's grip – beneath the great roof.

34

XIII

Hrothgar's gleeman or minstrel improvises a song to celebrate Beowulf's feat. He presents Sigemund, a hero of Scandinavian and Germanic legend, in an entirely successful light, though the audience will know of tragic undertones to the story. Heremod, the Danish king before Scyld, underlines the heroic comparison by contrast.

Then in the morning   was many a warrior   837–924
there in the gift-hall,   as I have heard tell.
Chieftains foregathered   from far and near,
travelled wide ways   to see the wonder,
the enemy's traces.   The end of his life
did not appear   grievous to any
who saw the footprints   of the infamous one:
how weary in spirit   on his way back,
fated and fugitive,   vanquished in fighting,
he dragged his tracks   to the water-demons' lake.
Surging with blood   was the water's brim,
a foul swirl of waves   hotly beswept
with gore, boiling   with battle's carnage.
Death-fated, stealing   through the fen's refuge,
joyless he laid   aside his life,
his heathen soul.   There hell received him.
  Old retainers   then turned back
from the track of triumph,   and a troop of the young,
wheeling horses from the lake,   proud at heart,
fine men on fair steeds.   Beowulf's great feat
was loudly acclaimed.   Many declared
and said it again,   that north and south
between the seas,   there was no better warrior
over all Earth   under sky's expanse,
no finer shield-bearer,   more fit for kingship.
Nor did they fault   their lord-friend at all,
the gracious Hrothgar: a good king was he.

35

At times hardy warriors   let their chestnut horses
cavort and gallop,   race in contest
where the earth-tracks,   famed for excellence,
offered good going.   At times a king's gleeman,
laden with eloquence,   who knew many lays
and had in mind   a vast multitude
of ancient tales,   found new turns of speech,
linked true and strong.   A song he started
of Beowulf's deed,   took it up deftly,
telling, re-telling   the aptest of tidings,
varying the words.   To the trials of valour
of Sigemund he turned,   the son of Waels,
setting forth all –   and much scarcely known –
he had heard tell   of Sigemund's travels.

To the sons of men   nothing had been said
of the foul crimes he suffered,   apart from Fitela,
to whom he had told   some of the tales,
uncle to nephew.   They were always,
in every affliction,   friends in need;
they had with their swords   slain a great number
of the race of giants.   For Sigemund there rose
at his life's end   no little glory,
when in brave combat   he killed the dragon
that guarded the hoard.   Under the grey rock
the son of the chieftain   set out alone –
not with Fitela –   on a deed fraught with risk.
It so fell out   that the sword struck through
the wondrous dragon,   till it wedged in the wall,
the mighty blade: the monster died bloodily.
The fearsome one reaped   the reward of courage:
the treasure-hoard   was his to enjoy
howsoever he wished.   The son of Waels
loaded a sea-boat,   bearing bright ornaments

to the ship's hold.   The dragon melted in heat.
He was the most famous   by far of adventurers
in the known world,   a protector of warriors;
his acts of valour   availed him well.
    Earlier Heremod   had lost all heart
for the battle-fray,   and so was betrayed
in the Jutes' kingdom   to enemy's keeping,
soon sent to his death.   Surges of sadness
had too long oppressed him;   he was to his people,
to all noble men,   a mortal sorrow.
Often and again,   in that time of old,
many a wise man   mourned his going.
They had hoped his daring   would end their distress,
that the son of the prince   would surely prosper,
take his father's high place   and preserve the people,
their treasure and stronghold,   the Scyldings' land,
a kingdom of heroes.   Hygelac's kinsman
gladdens all now,   his Géat companions
and every man.   Evil entered the other.

Still now and again   down the sandy tracks
they raced their mounts.   The morning light
rippled, ran forward.   Many a retainer
went bold-hearted   to the high hall
to see the strange wonder;   the king himself stepped out
from the queen's room.   Famed for high qualities,
the guardian of treasure-hoards   came forward glorious
with a great troop.   His good queen with him
took the mead-hall path   with a band of maidens.

XIV

The arm attached to a roof-beam inspires a speech of heartfelt thanks from Hrothgar and silence from Unferth (Ecglaf's son).

Hrothgar spoke —   he went to the hall,   925–990
stood on the steps,   and saw the high roof
adorned with gold   and with Grendel's arm:
    "For this fair sight   let thanks go swiftly
to the Almighty!   An awful affliction
was mine through Grendel —   may God the Defender
of Glory ever work   wonder on wonder!
It was but now   that I thought never
to live to see   a single sorrow
ever lifted,   when lying in blood
the best of houses   stood battle-gory,
a cruel grief   to my counsellors.
No hope had they   of ever holding
the people's fort   against such fiends
and monstrous spirits.   But now a man
by the Lord's power   has performed a deed
none of us   could ever achieve,
for all our skill.   Truly she may say —
and so any mother   who bore that son
in the legions of men —   if she still lives,
the Lord of Old   allowed his kindness
at her child-bearing.   Now Beowulf,
best of men,   in my heart I embrace you
as a son.   Keep sure and strong
this new kinship.   You shall lack nothing
you long for in life,   to the limit of my power.
Very often for less   have I vouchsafed treasure,
rewarding a less worthy   warrior with gifts,
one weaker in battle.   But by your brave deed
you have gained for yourself   a glorious name

38

to be treasured always.   May the Almighty
reward you with favour,   as he ever has done!"
   Beowulf spoke,   son of Ecgtheow:
"In full-hearted friendship   we performed
the warlike deed,   and dared to risk
the strange beast's strength.   Burdened with agony,
death-weary as he was,   I dearly wish
you could have seen   the suffering foe!
It was my aim   to engage him quickly
in the direst of holds   upon his death-bed;
to make him lie struggling   in the last throes
by the force of my grasp,   unless he got free.
I was not able,   the Lord willed it not,
to keep him from going,   my grip was too loose
on the deadly enemy;   exceeding strong
was he in his writhing.   Yet he rendered up
a hand for his life,   left it behind
with the arm and shoulder.   But he earned for himself,
the destitute creature,   no comfort by that.
The loathsome evil-doer   lives none the longer,
struck down by his sins,   but anguish constricts him
in its deadly vice,   within its violent
bonds of destruction.   He must abide
the great decree,   the crime-stained creature,
how the Lord in his majesty   judges him."
   Ecglaf's son   was more silent now
in his boastful talk   of battle-deeds,
as after the work   of the warrior, the nobles
looked up at the hand   by the high roof,
the foe's fingers.   At the front of each one
each single nail   was exactly like steel
in the heathen's claw,   the bloodthirsty creature's
terrible spikes.   Everyone said
no hard thing   was a threat to him,

no excellent blade   might ever have injured
the monster's bloody   battle-hand.

XV

Hrothulf is Hrothgar's nephew. At a later time (only alluded to in
Beowulf*) he is to attack his cousins for the throne.*

It was commanded   quickly that Heorot   991–1049
be decked out within;   men and women
were there in number   to renew the wine-building,
the hall of guests.   Gold-thread tapestries
glittered on the walls;   for all who gazed round
there was many   a marvellous sight.
The bright hall had been   all broken about,
though clamped on the inside   by iron clasps;
the door-hinges had started out;   only the roof stayed
all intact,   when with evil act stained,
the monster turned   and took to flight,
despairing of life.   It is no light thing
to retreat from fate,   let him try it who will.
Out of pure need   a person will come
at last to a place   for dwellers on land,
for those who bear souls,   for the sons of men,
where the body, set still   on a bed of rest,
sleeps after the feast.
                            Now the time was fitting
for Healfdene's son   to enter the hall;
the king was glad   to grace the banquet.
I have not heard tell   of a troop of men
who bore themselves better   about their liege lord.
In soaring spirits   they sat at the benches
to take their fill.   In gracious fashion
Hrothgar and Hrothulf,   mighty at heart,

tasted a measure   from many a mead-cup
in the high hall.   Heorot within
was filled with friends.   In the Danish family
no act of treachery   took place at that time.
   Healfdene's brave son   handed Beowulf
a golden ensign,   earned by the victory,
an adorned war-banner,   a breastplate and helmet;
and a famous rich sword   was seen to be borne
before the hero.   Beowulf drank
from the hall-cup: he had   no cause to hold back
before the warriors   at the bestowal.
I have not heard tell   of a handsome gift
of four golden treasures   given by many
to an ale-bench fellow   in as friendly a fashion.
At the helmet's crown   an outer rim held
the head-guard, bent round   with metal bands;
so that no filed sword,   storm-fierce and hard,
should too much shake him,   when the shield-warrior
against the enemy   needs must go.
And the people's king   called for eight horses
with bridles of gold   to be brought to the hall
and to stand within.   On one of them lay
a finely-wrought saddle,   rich, rare in adornment:
the high-born commander's   battle-seat,
when Healfdene's son   went seeking sword-play.
His far-famed valour   was always to the fore
at the war-front   when corpses were falling.
Forthwith the defender   of the Danes
presented all these   to Beowulf, and pressed him
to use both the war-gear   and horses well.
So finely then   did the famous prince,
treasure-holder for heroes,   reward battle's trial
with steeds and rich store,   such that one who seeks
to speak no falsehood   would never find fault with.

XVI

The minstrel's song here is clearly a well-known sad one. A long-standing feud between Danes and Frisians (or Jutes) is re-awakened in the Frisian king's hall. Both sides are weakened in the fighting and a stand-off ensues. Finally the Danes rally. Perhaps the song's underlying burden is to echo the tragedy of a conflict that appears never to end, as reflected in the figure of Hildeburh. The sister of Hnaef of the Scyldings (Danes) and wife of Finn of the Frisians, her song of mourning for her son seems to cry aloud with the grief of all who lose dear ones in war.

On all besides   who had set out by sea   1050–1124
along with Beowulf,   the Danish leader
bestowed a treasure   there at the mead-bench,
an heirloom; and gave   an order for gold
in return for the one   wickedly killed
before by Grendel.   More would be gone
if wise God had not   withheld that fate,
and for one man's courage.   The Lord had control
over humankind   and has it still.
And so understanding   is everywhere best
and forethought of mind.   Much can he expect,
whose stay is long   in these days of strife
upon the earth,   from enemy and friend.
   Songs were performed   and instruments played
before Healfdene's   battle-general.
The harp's tuneful wood   was tried, tales were told,
as Hrothgar's singer   set in motion
the hall's entertainment   about the mead-benches.

At the hands of Finn's men   in a swift foray
Hnaef of the Scyldings,   hero of the Half-Danes,
fell in a death-fight   with the Frisians.
Then Hildeburh had   no heart to praise

the Jutes' good faith;   the guiltless one
lost at shield-play   two she loved,
a son and a brother   brought to their doom
by the stab of the spear: a sad woman was she.
Not without cause   when morning came
did the daughter of Hoc   mourn fate's decree;
for she could see   under the sky
foul slaughter of kinsmen,   where before she had found
the most joy on earth.   All Finn's men
were felled in the fighting,   but for a poor few,
so that he could not   in any encounter
bring to an end   the battle with Hengest,
the follower of Hnaef,   nor by fighting dislodge
the sad day's survivors.   Hengest struck terms:
that another hall   and high seat of honour
should be readied for them,   where they might rule
on an equal standing   with the sons of Jutes.
A daily tribute   of treasure to the Danes
should be paid by Finn,   Folcwalda's son,
enriching Hengest's   troop with rings
and precious treasures   of plated gold,
to the same measure   that Finn was minded
to honour his Frisians   in the ale-hall.
Both sides then   were bound by treaty,
a strong compact of peace.   Finn swore solemn
oaths to Hengest   with open heart,
to seek good counsel   and aid the survivors
of the sad day.   He said that no-one
would break the treaty   by word or by deed,
nor speak of it ever   in spite or in malice,
though the Danes were subject   to their lord's slayer,
hard-pressed as they were,   with no prince to lead them.
If then a Frisian   in foolhardy speech
was mindful of   the murderous feud,

it fell to the sword's edge   to settle the matter.
*   The pyre was made ready,   and marvellous gold*
brought up from the hoard: the best of warriors
of the Battle-Scyldings   was set for burning.
Upon the pyre   plain to see
were gory mail-shirts,   gold-gleaming images
of the iron-hard boar.   Many heroes had fallen
fatally wounded,   men who died fighting.
Then Hildeburh ordered   that her own son
be given to the flame,   to the heat of Hnaef's fire,
his bone-vessel placed   on the pyre and burned.
In her sorrow   she sang at his shoulder
a song of mourning.   The warrior was set high;
the greatest of slaughter-fires   rose to the skies,
roared by the grave-mound.   Then heads melted,
wounds split and burst   as blood spilt forth
out of grim gashes.   Greediest of spirits,
the flame consumed all   carried off by war
of either people.   Their prowess was no more.

XVII

The setting in the lament of a past sadness could not be further removed from the situation of two peoples sharing a joyous closeness at the present time. The sense of the transience of all things, that is at the heart of the Anglo-Saxon poetic mind, is left in the air. On the surface the song ends, appropriately enough, with a Danish victory; yet an underlying havoc, as it seems, is ever-present. Blind forces of destruction, together with a welcome restoration in the natural and the human world, add a depth to the scene (that is itself covertly ironic with the queen's trust in her nephew Hrothulf).

*   Guthlaf and Oslaf are Danes who instigate a delayed counter-attack against Finn.*

With many friends lost,   to the Frisian land   1125–1191
Finn's warriors departed   to see their dwellings,
their homes and high forts.   Hengest still
stayed near Finn   in sheer misfortune
that slaughter-stained winter.   His heart set on home,
he could not run   the ring-prowed ship
down onto the water.   The sea welled with storm,
strove with the wind;   winter locked the waves,
sealed them with ice.   At last a new spring
came to the dwellings,   as it does still,
the glorious light air   that always arrives
to see out its season.   The winter was shaken off,
the earth's lap lovely.   The exiled guest
ached to be away.   His every thought
was not on the voyage,   but to avenge his wrong.
He craved to return   to a raging encounter,
to seek a reckoning   with the sons of the Jutes.
So he did not deny   the dictates of custom,
when Hunlafing laid   upon his lap
a light of battle,   the best of blades;
among the Jutes   the edge was a legend.
A fierce sword-death   later befell
Finn the brave-hearted   in his own home.
Back from a sea-going,   Guthlaf and Oslaf
made a loud outcry   about the attack,
chanting their woes;   nor could their charged spirits
stay still in their breasts.   The hall was stained
with the life-blood of enemies.   So Finn was laid low,
the king in his troop,   and the queen taken.
The Scylding warriors   bore to the ships
all the belongings   of the lord of the land,
whatever in Finn's home   they could find
of jewels and dear treasure.   Then by sea-journey
to the Danes they led   the illustrious lady,
to her own people.

The old song was sung,
the minstrel's lay.   Mirth rose again,
the bench-din sounded,   bearers served wine
from glorious vessels.   In a gold crown
Wealhtheow came up   to the two kingly men,
paternal uncle and nephew,   still now at peace,
the one true to the other.   Unferth sat as advisor
at the Scylding lord's feet;   then all had faith
in his fine spirit   despite his dishonour
to his kinsmen in sword-play.   The Scylding queen spoke:
"Take this cup,   my noble commander,
giver of treasure;   be you glad,
gold-friend of men,   and speak to the Géats
some gentle words,   and justly so.
Be gracious to them: have a thought to the gifts
that now are yours   from far and near.
They say you hold him   as a son,
the battle-hero.   Heorot is cleansed,
the shining ring-hall: a rich reward
furnish as you may.   And when you go forth
to fate's decree,   entrust to your family
your folk and your realm.   I know full well
my good, true Hrothulf   is sure to treat
the youngsters fitly,   if before him,
lord of the Scyldings,   you leave the world.
Right royally   he will repay
our sons, when once   he summons to mind
all the benefits   he had as a boy
from the pair of us,   for his pleasure and honour."
She turned to the seat   where her boys sat,
Hrethric and Hrothmund   with sons of heroes,
the troop's youthful men.   The trusty warrior,
Beowulf the Géat,   sat with the two brothers.

XVIII

There were many legends of stolen treasure. As often as not there is a curse attached to it. Here the narrator's digression on the magic necklace of the Brisings nicely suggests the hubbub in the hall at the magnificent gifts, all brought to order by the queen's calm and measured words.

Though his death is referred to here, Hygelac (Swerting's descendant) is alive at this point in the chain of events. For the sake of the necklace detail the poet allows himself to be a little ahead of himself. One assumes his audience, familiar with the essence, is not put out.

To him the brimming cup was borne   1192–1250
with friendly words; and finely-worked gold
was offered, two arm-ornaments,
a corslet and rings, and the richest neck-collar,
as I am told, upon the earth.
Such hoard-gems of heroes I have not heard of
under the sky, since Hama absconded
to the bright fortress with the Brisings' necklace,
the bejewelled torque. He took lifelong gains
and escaped Eormenric's arts of battle.
Hygelac of the Géats had the neck-collar with him
in his last deed of daring. Swerting's descendant
defended the war-booty under the banner,
fought for his riches. Fate took him off
when in his pride he pressed towards trouble,
a feud with the Frisians. He had fetched treasure,
bright stones over the waves' brimming cup,
a stalwart leader. He sank beneath the shield.
The king's body passed to the Franks' keeping,
his coat-of-mail, the collar besides;
lesser warriors looted the corpses
after the slaughter. Géats lay slain
on the death-strewn ground. Now a din filled the hall.

47

Wealhtheow spoke then   before the throng:
"Be glad of this collar,   beloved Beowulf,
young man of fortune,   make use of this corslet,
the wealth of this people,   and prosper well,
bear yourself finely.   Be to my boys
a thoughtful instructor   and earn my thanks more.
You have brought it to pass   that men will praise you
far and near   for ever and ever,
even as widely   as the sea embraces
the wind's home, the heights.   Warrior, be happy
as long as you live!   Let there be treasure
for you in abundance.   Be to my sons
generous in act,   bearer of joy!
Here each man   holds faith with his fellow,
is mild in temper   and true to his lord;
this ready band   of revelling warriors
is ever at one   and obedient to me."

    She went to her seat.   A superb feast took place;
the men drank wine   not knowing their destiny,
the fierce ancient decree   already in force
for the troop of nobles   at coming of night.
Hrothgar departed   to his dwelling,
the king to his rest.   A crowd of his men
occupied the hall   as often earlier.
Benches were moved back;   with beds and cushions
the floor was festooned.   With his fate all too near
one of the beer-drinkers   lay on his hall-bed.
They set at their heads   the shields of war,
the bright wooden bucklers.   There on the bench
above each noble   in open view
lay the ringed breastplate,   the battle-tall helmet,
the strong-wood spear.   It was their way,
the warriors' custom   to have war-gear waiting,
whenever their liege lord   might lie in need,

out in the field   or else at home,
in either event.   An excellent troop!

XIX

*Given the benighted origin of the Grendel clan, it is touching to find
the stern moraliser within the poet come out with a gentler aphorism ('A
bad bargain...'). The monster's mother, a mythic creation that seems to
tap into an atavistic sense of raw female ferocity, is allowed a fleeting
moment of understanding on the reader's part, not far short of compas-
sion. A vanishing speck: but it may allow the man-monster conflict not
to be entirely distanced from the poem's backcloth of inter-tribal strife.
Evil exists, in the poet's broad view; and yet a hint escapes (it may be)
that nothing is entirely "black-and-white". In more than one way it is
a complex story.*

They sank into sleep.   One paid sorely   1251–1320
for his evening-slumber,   as often and again
it had been when Grendel   held sway in the gold-hall,
evil in his ways   till the end came,
death after crime.   It became all too clear,
and was told far and wide   for a grievous time,
that one to avenge   had survived the enemy
beyond the grim struggle.   Grendel's mother,
a monstrous female,   bore her misery in mind.
She was doomed to dwell   in direful streams,
ice-cold currents,   because of Cain,
the slayer by sword   of his father's son,
his only brother.   In blood-guilt he left,
marked by the killing,   to lose joys of men
and live in the wasteland.   From there awoke
a great host of the doomed.   One such was Grendel,
the hateful cursed foe,   who found at Heorot
a man keeping watch   and waiting for battle.

49

The monster grabbed him,   grappling closely;
but calling to mind   the power of his might,
the splendid gift given   to him by God,
and in the One Ruler   resting his trust
for comfort and aid,   he overcame the enemy,
subdued the hell-spirit.   The assailant of men
was made to retreat,   wretched and joyless,
to look on death's home.   With murder at heart
the ravening mother   resolved to make
a dismal journey   to avenge her son's death.
  So she reached Heorot,   with the Ring-Danes asleep
inside the hall.   Everything altered
at once for the men   as Grendel's mother
stepped inside.   By just so much
was the terror less keen   as a woman's war-craft,
her fearsome might,   is less than a man's,
when the embellished sword   with hammer-beaten
scything blade,   all stained with blood,
cuts through the boar-crest   above the foe's helmet.
Then in the hall   the hard-edge was out,
swords above benches.   Many a broad shield
was clenched in the hand.   None remembered his helmet
or hefty breastplate   as the horror took hold.
  She moved in haste,   intent to make off,
to save her life   when she was seen.
Swiftly she seized   a certain warrior,
laying fast hold   as she turned to the fen.
He was to Hrothgar   the dearest of heroes
between the seas,   a mighty shield-warrior,
a companion in rank   of broad renown,
whom she killed on the bed.   Beowulf was elsewhere,
in another place   earlier assigned
after the giving of gifts   to the noble Géat.
And she took the famed hand   that was fouled with gore.

There was uproar in Heorot.   Sorrow was reborn
about the building.   A bad bargain it was
when either party   had to pay
with a loved one's life.   The venerable lord,
the grey battle-warrior   grieved at heart,
when he came to know   the noble retainer
had departed his life,   the dearest one dead.
   Quickly Beowulf   was brought to the hall,
the victory-hero.   Dawn touched the heaven
as the noble one came   with his companions
to where the wise one,   the king, was waiting
to see if the Almighty   at last might allow
a turn for the better   after tidings of woe.
With his band about him   the battle-honoured man
went down the floor –   the hall-wood dinned –
to go and salute   the leader in words,
the king of Ing's people.   Called out so early,
he asked him – had he   enjoyed a good night?

XX

A haunting atmosphere surrounds the tales of Grendel and his mother.

Hrothgar spoke,   the Scyldings' protector: 1321–1382
"Ask not after joy;   sorrow again
has come to the Danes.   Aeschere is dead,
the elder brother of   Yrmenlaf,
my counsellor   and close advisor,
the friend at my shoulder   when we fought
to keep our heads safe,   when foot-soldiers clashed
and smote the boar-crests.   So should a man be
as Aeschere was,   a noble outstanding!
Here in Heorot   he was killed by the hand
of a death-roaming demon.   I do not know where

the proud one,   glorying in her prey,
all-terrible in her food,   has returned to.
It was for Grendel's   grim fate last night
from your fierce hand-grip   of such force.
After his many   assaults on my people,
laying them waste,   he gave way in the battle
and forfeited life.   But a foe has come,
evil in power,   to avenge her son.
She has taken   a heavy toll,
as it will seem   to many a warrior
who grieves in his heart   for the ring-giver
with a hard sorrow.   Now the hand is laid low
that once would fulfil   all that you wished for.
    "I heard it said   by counsellors in hall
that there were men   among my people
who saw a pair   of such great power,
border-walkers   stalking the moor-wastes,
alien spirits.   Of the two strangers
one, as surely   as they could say,
appeared a female,   in man's form the other;
wretched shapes treading   the tracks of exile;
but the male was bigger   than any man.
In days gone by   he was named Grendel
by the folk of the district.   They know not of a father,
or if he might earlier   have spawned another
strange alien thing.   A secret land
is theirs, wolf-slopes   and wind-swept headlands,
a treacherous marsh-path.   A mountain-stream
runs away down   in the cliff's dark mist
to an underground flood.   Not far from here,
to measure in miles,   a lake remains,
with frosted groves   leaning over the face,
the deep-set trees   overshadowing it.
A terrible wonder   each night may be witnessed,

fire on water.   In the family of man
none is so wise   as to know what is down there.
Though the heath-stalker,   harassed by dogs,
the antler-strong stag   may seek the forest
in flight from afar,   he will die first,
lose his life on the bank,   before he will lower
his head to that pool.   It is no happy spot.
The waves climb up   black under the clouds,
thrown in turmoil   when the wind thrashes
in enemy storms,   till the air chokes with mist,
the heavens weep.   Again our help
is from you alone.   It is unknown to you,
the dangerous haunt   where you may discover
the deep-sinning creature.   Seek it if you dare!
I shall reward   the raid with riches,
with ancient treasures   as I did earlier,
with twisted gold,   if you go and come back."

XXI

The description of the sword Hrunting almost lays a spell on the proceedings, regardless of the use made of it; and so with a number of items of weaponry and armour in the story.

Beowulf spoke,   son of Ecgtheow,   1383–1472
"Sorrow not, wise one!   To seek revenge
for a friend is more fitting   than to mourn overmuch.
Each of us must   endure the end
of his life in the world.   Let him who may win
distinction before death: that is indeed best
for a man of worth   when his life is no more.
Rise, realm-protector,   let us be ready
to trace Grendel's mother   in her tracks.
I swear this to you: no shelter shall hide her,

not the earth's embrace,   nor the ocean's depths,
nor the mountainous wood,   let her go where she may.
On this day   be patient then
in the depth of your woe,   as I know that you will."
    The old one leapt up   and offered thanks
to mighty Lord God   for the man's words.
The prince's horse   of plaited mane
was held and bridled.   Hrothgar rode out
splendid at the fore   as the foot-troop marched
armed with shields.   The line of the spoor
lay straight and direct   along the ground,
visible far   down forest-paths,
to the dark moor.   She took the dead body
of the very best   of the band of youth
who with Hrothgar   had guarded the homeland.
The son of princes   pressed on out
over cliffs of rock,   along closed-in paths,
winding in single file   over strange ways,
past the homes   of a host of water-demons.
He went ahead   together with
a few shrewd men   to spy out the place;
and then he suddenly   caught sight
of hill-trees stooping   over grey stone,
a joyless wood.   Water lay below,
blood-stained, disturbed.   In the Danish force,
in the king's followers,   minds were fraught
with suffering.   Each single man
was in distress   as he discovered
Aeschere's head   by the high lake.
    The flood was heaving   with blood and hot gore.
They gazed. The horn   again, again
sang the quick song of battle.   The foot-troop sat:
in the lake they saw many   of the serpent kind,
strange sea-demons   searching the water.

On the head-slopes as well   water-serpents lay,
wild creatures and monsters   that often commit
deeds on the sail-road   when the day is young
that lead to great sorrow.   They submerged and sank,
enraged and bitter   at the brilliant sound
of the war-horn's singing.   The Weder-Géat chief
with arrow and bow   parted one from its being,
severed from its wave-work;   the hard war-shaft
had lodged in its vitals.   Now in the lake
it was slower at swimming,   since death took it off.
Quickly in the waves   with questing boar-spears
it was beset,   brutally hooked
and tightly trapped,   a wondrous wave-traveller
hauled out to the headland.   The men beheld
the horror in their midst.

                         Beowulf girded himself
in warrior's armour,   unafraid.
His corslet-of-war,   hand-linked and wide,
skilfully styled,   was to seek out the waters.
It was a barrier   about the bone-chamber
to stop a battle-hold   harming his heart,
a fierce angry grip   endangering life.
The shining helmet   guarding his head,
that was soon to disturb   the deep bed of the lake
and try its turmoil,   was set with treasures,
adorned all about   with rich bands of old.
The weapon-smith's work   had wonderfully circled it
with boar-figures round,   so that no blade,
no sword of battle   might later slice it.
By no means the least   of his mighty aids
was one lent by Unferth,   Hrothgar's advisor.
Hrunting was the name   of his long-hilted blade,
a rich and rare treasure   from times of old.
The iron sword, shining   with venomous serpent-shapes,

hardened with blood-sweat   of battle, had failed
none in the fray   whose fist had enclosed it,
who had dared to go off   on a dangerous errand
to face the enemy.   It was not the first time
it had been borne off   to a brave deed.

   The son of Ecglaf,   mighty in strength,
had surely forgotten   his wine-drunken speech
of before, when he lent   his battle-weapon
to a braver swordsman.   He himself was not bold
to risk his life under   the rack of waves
in a noble act.   There he lost his good name,
a warrior's esteem.   It was not so with the other,
when he had fitted   himself for the fray.

XXII

To translate hringa þengel *as the lord of the rings is a translator's
indulgence, though it is the literal meaning. It is almost bound to be a
reference to Beowulf's fine chain-mail armour. If J.R.R. Tolkien, who
was far more than a scholar of the poem, took the title for his trilogy
from the phrase, to keep his wording is in the nature of a somewhat
chancy tribute.*

Beowulf spoke,   son of Ecgtheow: 1473–1556
"Cast back your mind,   gold-friend of men,
son of Healfdene,   to what was said earlier,
renowned and wise king,   for now I am ready
to dare the deed.   If I am to die
addressing your need,   you will be always
in a father's place   when I am gone forth.
Be you a protector   to my young troop,
the friends of my bosom,   should battle take me;
likewise the rich gifts   that you gave me,
beloved Hrothgar,   send to Hygelac.

The lord of the Géats   may know from the gold,
Hrethel's son see   as he stares at the riches,
that I found a good man,   a giver of treasure,
and enjoyed his high bounty   as I was able.
And let Unferth take   the ancient relic,
my wave-frilled sword.   The far-famed one
can keep the hard-edge.   I will with Hrunting
do a deed of glory,   or death will take me."
    After these words   the Weder-Géat chief
hurried on eagerly,   all unwilling
to wait for an answer.   The wave-surge embraced
the battle-warrior.   A long time went by
before he could make out   the bottom-most depths.
    At once she saw,   whom the flood's wide expanse
had held for a hundred   half-years, a fierce fighter,
greedy, murderous,   that one of the men
from above had entered   the alien beasts' home.
She clutched at him   with terrible claws,
seizing the warrior;   yet none the sooner
was the strong body harmed   by those hostile fingers.
She could not break   the battle-covering,
the interlocked ring-mail   binding him round.
Then she went deep,   the she-wolf of the waters,
bore the lord of the rings   to her abode;
in her clasp for all   his courage he could not
brandish his weapons.   A host of strange beasts
harassed him swimming;   many a sea-monster
with battle-tusks cracked   his corslet-of-war,
chasing the hero.   The chieftain saw
that he had entered   some enemy hall
where no water   in any way harmed him.
The roofed hall saved him   from being swamped
by the flood's swift reach.   A flash of fire
he saw, a gleam-glow   brightly glittering.

The hero could see   the accursed creature,
the mighty mere-woman.   Massively he swung
the blade and did not   hold back his hand;
the ringed sword eagerly   sang its battle-song
about her head.   But the hall-guest found
there was no way   the war-torch would cut
to injure life.   The edge betrayed
the noble in his need.   It had known many
hand-to-hand meetings,   sheared many helmets,
the armour of fated ones;   this was the first time
the fair costly treasure   failed in its fame.

Again determined,   remembering great deeds,
Hygelac's kinsman   lost none of his courage.
The angry warrior   threw away the sword
of circling ornament;   strong and steel-edged
it lay on the ground.   In the strength of his hand-grip,
his own might, he trusted.   The man who is minded
to win a name   of lasting renown
in the fray can set   no store on his life.
The Géat chief   seized Grendel's mother
by the shoulder, reckless   of her wrath;
and in fierce attack,   swelling in fury,
flung the deadly enemy   who dropped to the floor.
Quickly in turn   she requited him,
grabbing at him   with a cruel grasp.
Weary in spirit   the strongest of warriors,
fighting on foot,   stumbled and fell.
She knelt on the stranger: a shining, broad knife-blade
now she drew out.   For her only offspring
she longed for revenge.   On his shoulders lay
the interlocked mail-shirt   that saved his life,
withstood the piercing   by point and blade.
Ecgtheow's son   would have met his end,
the Géat champion   in the deep roomy chamber,

if his battle-harness   had not been of help,
the hard war-netting;   and if holy God,
the wise Lord, had not   wielded his victory.
Again he stood up.   Easily then
did the Ruler of the Skies   judge the issue aright.

XXIII

The second great deed is done.

A victory-rich sword   in some war-gear he saw,   1557–1650
an old blade, mighty   of edge, made by giants,
a worthy war-relic,   the best of weapons
but for being larger   than could be borne
by any other person   to the battle-play –
magnificent, noble,   massively shaped.
The Scyldings' champion   seized the whorled hilt
in a savage rage,   and swung the ringed sword
in despair of his life.   In livid fury he struck,
and with a great knock   it fastened on her neck,
breaking the bone-rings;   the blade went right through
the doomed frame of flesh.   She fell dead on the floor;
gore covered the sword.   He was glad of the deed.
    The fiery light flamed   and flashed down there,
even as heaven's candle   casts a clear light
out of the skies.   His eyes scanned the room;
then Hygelac's warrior   turned to the wall,
savage, single-minded,   raising the sword
hard by the hilt.   No small help was the blade
to the man of battle,   for now he meant
to repay Grendel   for all the raids
he had undertaken   against the Danes.
Far more had there been   since the first foray,
when he struck at Hrothgar's   hearth-companions

as they slept, devouring   in their slumber
fifteen retainers   of the Danish realm,
and carrying off   an equal number –
awful pickings.   He paid him well,
the fierce fighter,   when he found Grendel,
the battle-tired body   still on its death-bed,
all life gone   with the earlier hurt
in the clash at Heorot.   The corpse burst wide open
as after death   it endured a dire blow,
a hard swing of the sword,   as he sliced off the head.
    At once they saw,   the watchful men
with Hrothgar locking   their eyes on the lake,
a sudden turmoil   of mounting waves
all stained with gore.   Of the good man
the old and grey-haired   spoke together;
they said they held   no hope for the hero,
of his ever coming   before the great king
to tell of a triumph.   It seemed true to many
the she-wolf of the waters   had laid him waste.
It was the day's ninth hour.   The noble Danes left
the headland ground;   the gold-friend of men
set off for home.   The visitors sat
sick at heart   and stared at the lake,
hopelessly longing   to see their dear leader
in person himself.
                        Now the sword started,
the blade of combat,   to shrink with blood-sweat
into war-icicles.   It was a wonder –
it all melted   away like ice,
when the Father loosens   the fetters of frost,
unwinds the water-ropes,   the one Ruler
of times and seasons,   the true certain Lord.
The Weder-Géat hero   took from the hall
no more spoil   though much was there,

but only the head   and the sword-hilt with it,
richly adorned.   The damascened blade
had burned away, melted,   the blood was so hot,
so deadly the alien   spirit that died.
At once he was swimming,   who had survived
where his foes perished,   pressing on up.
All the wave-medley   was purged within
its vast expanse   as the alien spirit
departed its days   and the passing world.
    Swimming stout-heartedly,   the seafarers' guardian
gained the shore;   he was glad of his booty,
the mighty burden   he had brought with him.
They went to him then,   the fine warrior band,
giving thanks to God.   They took great joy
in seeing their chieftain   safe and sound.
Helmet and corslet   from the hardy body
were swiftly stripped.   Stained with death's blood
the lake-water settled   below the sky.
Then they went forth   along the foot-paths
triumphant at heart,   treading the earth-tracks
they knew from before.   As bold as kings
men carried the head   from the cliff by the mere,
a strenuous task   for the brave stalwarts,
testing each one.   It took the labour
of four to bear it   on a battle-shaft,
to bring to the gold-hall   Grendel's head.
So they made haste   to the hall,
marching brave   and battle-keen,
the fourteen Géats.   The great-hearted noble
trod with his men   the mead-hall fields.
The warrior chief   went on and in,
the man of brave deeds,   the daring hero
with a name of glory,   and greeted Hrothgar.
Then by the hair   Grendel's head

was dragged in the hall   where men were drinking,
a monstrous thing   to the men and the lady,
a fearful spectacle   that they stared at.

XXIV

Again we hear of Heremod, the last Danish king before the Scyld dynasty. Hrothgar appears to advise Beowulf on the perils and responsibilities of kingship.

The son of Ecgtheow,   Beowulf, spoke: 1651–1739
"Look, son of Healfdene.   This lake-booty,
great king of the Danes,   that you gaze at now,
we bring you gladly   as a sign of glory.
Not easily did I   escape with my life
the underwater attack.   To take on that task
was a hard thing indeed.   Had God not defended me,
in a trice it would all have been   over and done with.
Nor was Hrunting   the slightest help
in the fray, a weapon   of worth though it be;
but the Ruler of men   granted it me
to see a beautiful   huge old sword
hanging on the wall –   so often has he lent
direction to the lost –   and I drew the weapon.
When my chance came,   on those hall-keepers
I dealt blows of death.   The damascened sword,
the keen blade burnt up   as the blood burst out,
the seething battle-gore.   I bore off the hilt
from the place of enemies.   I avenged evil deeds,
the foul slaughter of Danes,   as it was fitting.
And now I swear   you will know in Heorot
an untormented   sleep with your troop,
and so all your followers,   old and young,
within your land.   Leader of the Scyldings,

no more need you fear   a foul loss of life
from the direction   you did earlier."
    Into the hand   of the old man,
the grey battle-chief,   he set the gold hilt,
the old work of giants.   Into the ownership
of the king of the Danes,   now the demons had gone,
it passed, the creation   of cunning craftsmen.
When God's adversary   abandoned the world,
the murderous foe   and his mother too,
it fell to the hand   of the finest and best
of world-sovereigns   between the seas
who shared out treasure   in Scandinavia.
    Hrothgar spoke.   He looked at the hilt,
the ancient relic.   On it the origin
was cut of the old strife,   when the flood slew
the race of giants   in a rolling sea.
Fearful was their plight,   a people foreign
to the eternal Lord: the Ruler allowed them
their full reward   in the whirling waters.
And it was properly   marked on the hilt-plates
in runic letters   of lustrous gold,
saying for whom   the sword was made,
the best of iron-blades.   The hilt was embellished
with a spiral serpent.   The leader spoke out,
Healfdene's son,   and all were silent.
"An old ruler   who pursues rightness
and truth in his realm,   who remembers far back,
now surely can say   this noble man
was born to greatness!   My friend Beowulf,
your fame is high   over far regions
in every people.   You possess all with patience,
your might, your mind's wisdom.   I shall keep my word
of friendship as promised.   A full long age
shall you become   a solace to your kingdom,
a help to heroes.

"Such was not Heremod
to Ecgwela's issue,   to the Ar-Scyldings;
he did not turn out   to the Danes' liking,
for he was their downfall,   their slaughter-filled fate.
In rage he brought ruin   on his board-companions,
his shoulder-close allies,   till he went off alone,
the famous prince,   from the pleasures of men,
though granted great power   by the might of God
who exalted him   above all others,
holding him high.   But his heart's spirit harboured
a lust for blood.   He bestowed no treasures
on the Danes, to gain glory;   but lived without gladness,
oppressed by cares   from the trouble he caused,
the land's long evil.   Now learn from this
what is truly noble!   I tell you this tale,
wise in my years.
                    "It is a wonder to say
how mighty God   grants his gifts to mankind,
wisdom to some,   to some wealth and rank,
in his far seeing.   He has oversight of all.
Sometimes he permits   a man of proud place
to fix his thoughts   on his own fine position,
and gives him a kingdom   in his own country
to rule and protect,   a people's stronghold.
And parts of the world   he will place in his power,
a wide-reaching realm,   so that in his unwisdom
the man himself   cannot see an end.
He dwells in abundance,   nothing bars the way,
old age nor disease.   The ills of dark malice
do not enter his mind.   Nowhere does enmity
announce its sword-hatred;   but the whole world
bends to his will.

XXV

A sense of the strife of the dark past, as well as of the triumphs and tribulations of his own reign, informs Hrothgar's speech. As with Beowulf's final words at the story's end, a certain tenor is added to the poem, of great strength and frailty together; or in the simplest and deepest terms, the voice of experience.

"He knows nothing worse,   1739–1816
until inside him   a certain arrogance
grows and blossoms,   as the guard slumbers,
the keeper of the soul.   That sleep is too deep,
in worldly care sealed,   the slayer all too near
with evil intent   in his bow and arrow.
Then in the heart   he is hit, past protecting –
he has no defence –   by a fierce shaft,
the strange promptings   of the perverse spirit.
What he has held too long   seems too little to him;
greedy and angry   he gives no gold treasure
as honour bids,   but he overlooks
his future fate   for what God gave before,
the Guardian of heaven: his own worldly glory.
Afterwards comes   the final act:
the fleeting body-frame   falls away,
sinks to its doom.   Another takes his seat,
to give out riches   with no regret,
the fine old treasures   with no trace of fear.
Defend against this,   my dear Beowulf,
best of men;   choose the better part,
eternal benefit;   turn your back on pride,
famous warrior!   Now the majesty of your might
endures awhile;   but all too soon
sickness or the sword   will part you and your strength,
the flood's force   or the arms of the fire,
the gripped sword   or the hurled spear,

or grim old age.   Gleaming eyes
grow dim and dark.   Glorious warrior,
death will all at once   destroy you.
    "So have I ruled   the Ring-Danes on earth
a hundred half-years,   and held them safe
in war from tribes   around this world,
from spear and sword,   till I saw myself
free of enemies   under heaven.
Ah, a change came   over the kingdom,
grief after gladness,   the moment Grendel,
man's enemy of old,   ventured against me.
Over and over   I took from his visits
a great heart-sorrow.   Thanks be to God,
the eternal Lord,   I have lived to see this.
After long hardship,   at last at a head
covered with sword-gore   I gaze with my eyes!
Go now to the bench,   honoured in battle,
take joy of the feast!   A fine sharing-out
of a mass of treasure   will be ours in the morning."
    With a light heart   the Géat hero went
at once to his seat,   as the wise man had said.
Then again as before   a banquet was spread,
and a glad time was held   by those seated in hall,
famed for their courage.   Night's cover deepened
dark over the warriors.   The worthy men rose;
the grey-haired one wished   to go to his bed,
the aged Scylding.   The Géat too sought rest,
the excellent shield-man,   utterly tired.
At once a hall-servant   escorted him out,
the stranger from afar,   fatigued by the trial;
the servant in courtesy   saw to all
the warrior's wishes,   as for a sea-wanderer
in that day and age   it was the due.

The great-heart rested; the high hall towered
gold-adorned, spacious; the guest slept within,
till a black raven blithely announced
the delight of the skies. A lustre sped out
shining from darkness. The warriors stirred themselves;
the men were eager to be out and away
to their people and land. The bold visitor longed
to get back to his ship that lay some way off.
The hardy man ordered Hrunting to be borne
to Ecglaf's son, Unferth. He asked him to take back
his illustrious sword, giving thanks for the loan;
he said he reckoned it a ready friend in war,
mighty in battle. No blame for the blade's edge
did he at all hint at, a man of true heart.
The men were in armour and eager to go.
Then their champion, whom the Danes cherished,
went to the high seat where the other was,
and the battle-brave hero greeted Hrothgar.

XXVI

*We are left with a subtle contrast between the young noble and the old
king.*

Beowulf spoke, son of Ecgtheow: 1817–1887
"Now we seafarers from afar
confess that we are keen at heart
to return to Hygelac. You received us here
with grace and honour. You have been good to us.
If then on Earth in any way,
lord of men, I can earn more
of your heart's love than I have now,
I shall at once as a warrior be ready.
If I find out over the flood's way

67

that a neighbouring tribe   is troubling you –
such an enemy   as you have endured –
I shall bring a thousand   men to do battle,
heroes to your help.   As for Hygelac,
prince of the Géats,   the people's protector,
he is still young,   yet he will support me
in word and deed.   I shall do you honour
and supply to your aid   the shaft of the spear,
and shore up your strength   if you seek men.
If the royal prince Hrethric   has a purpose to see
the court of the Géats,   he will find that he gains
a host of friends there.   A far-off land
profits a traveller   of true worth himself."
Hrothgar said   to him in answer:
"The Lord in his wisdom   sends these words
into your heart.   I never heard a man
speak with such import   at so young an age.
You are strong in might   and wise in mind,
prudent of speech.   If so it be
that the spear or the sword   take Hrethel's son
in blade-fierce battle,   or else a fever
claim your prince,   the people's guardian,
and you have your life,   I think it likely
that the Sea-Géats   can select
none better than you   to be their king
and treasure-keeper for heroes,   if you are content
to take command.   Your character and spirit
delight me more and more,   my dear Beowulf.
With your action   all feuding is over
and peace has come   upon our peoples,
the Géat nation   and the Gar-Danes;
the strife is ended   they suffered before.
As long as I rule   there shall be open realm,
an exchange of rich gifts.   Across the gannet's bath

68

many will greet   a friend with good things.
The ring-prowed boat   will bring over the sea
precious tokens of love.   I know our peoples
are framed to be steadfast   with friend as with foe,
and blameless in all   in the old way."
    To him in the hall then   Healfdene's son,
the protector of men,   presented twelve gifts,
and told him to take them   and travel home safely
to his dear country,   and come back soon.
The noble king   of the Scyldings clasped
the best of warriors   about the neck
and kissed him then;   tears cascaded
from his grey head.   The good old wise man
saw two outcomes,   but the second more clearly:
that they would not talk   together again,
the two brave men.   So much did he care for him,
he could not hold back   a surging of the breast;
for locked away fast   in the fetters of his heart,
a hidden fondness   for the dear hero
burned in his blood.   Away from him Beowulf
trod the grassy ground,   a gold-proud warrior,
gladly adorned.   The sea-goer awaited
its owner and master,   riding at anchor.
As they approached it   the prince's rich gifts
were often acclaimed.   That was a king
in all quite blameless,   till old age, that often
does harm, denied him   the delight of his powers.

XXVII

*Offa's queen is brought in as a legend in her own right, and as an illus-
trative companion character to Hygd (after the manner of Unferth in
VIII and Heremod in XIII and XXIV). Her introduction allows the
poem a nod to Offa, the king of the Continental Angles in (perhaps) the
fourth century AD, and ancestor of Offa, the eighth-century king of the
English realm of Mercia.*

They came to the flood,   the fine courageous   1888–1962
body of young men,   with their coats-of-mail
of rings interlocking.   The coastguard remembered
the troop coming back   from seeing them before;
and from the cliff's headland   he hailed the visitors
with no hint of challenge,   but turned his horse to them.
The ship-bound warriors   in shining armour
he said would be welcomed   by the Weder people.
Then the boat on the shore,   broad-based for the sea,
the ring-prow was packed   with the raiment of war,
with treasure and horses.   The mast towered
over Hrothgar's   hoard of valuables.
   Beowulf gave   a sword to the boat-guard
embellished with gold;   after at the mead-bench
the man was more honoured   for the ownership
of the rich heirloom.   The boat went off out
from the land of the Danes   to disturb the deep waters.
Then at the mast   a sail, the sea's garment,
was secured with a rope;   the sea-wood groaned;
on the billows the wind did not   shift the boat's steering
as it bobbed the waves.   The sea-goer went well,
foamy-necked floating   forward on the current,
the strong-prowed ship   on the ocean's stream,
until they could see   the cliffs of the Géats,
the familiar shore-hills.   It shot on up,
the breeze at its back,   till it beached on land.

At the waterside   the watchman was ready.
For long he had scanned   the sea for a sighting
of the dear men.   Now he moored
the roomy ship   fast on the sand
with anchor-cables,   to keep the waves
from hauling off   the handsome vessel.
Beowulf gave orders   for the rich gifts,
the gold-plated treasures   to be taken up.
It was not far to go   to the giver of bounty,
to where Hygelac,   son of Hrethel,
lived near the sea's edge   with his nobles.
   The dwelling was magnificent   and the hall mighty.
It housed the famed king   and his wife Hygd,
well-accomplished and wise.   Not many winters
had she dwelt in the stronghold,   the daughter of Haereth,
young in years.   Yet she knew queenly ways,
no niggard was she;   to the Géat people
she offered treasure.   Unlike that other one,
rarest of queens,   who at first was quite wicked.
No brave man   among her retainers
dared be so bold,   not being her husband,
as to look directly   at her by day;
for he could count on   the corded death-rope
ordered for him;   and then right after
his body's arrest   and tying up for the blade,
the damascened sword   would settle it,
reveal its death-power.   It is not a queen's part,
for a lady to perform,   though she be peerless,
for a weaver of peace   to pluck the life
of a beloved man   in lying anger.
But a kinsman of Hemming   put a halt to all that.
Ale-drinkers said   who passed on the story,
her ill-will died   and she was no danger
to people, once   she had been presented,

decked in gold,   to a young gallant,
a most valued noble,   after a voyage
to Offa's hall   at her father's order
over the pale-gold sea.   For her royal goodness
she became famous,   and followed through life
her appointed fate   most profitably.
A noble love   she bore for her lord,
who as I heard   was the highest in excellence
of the race of the mighty   in all mankind
amid the oceans.   In truth Offa
was famed far and wide   for his gifts and his wars,
a ready spear-man,   who ruled his land wisely.
A son he had born,   a help to heroes,
Eomer, the latest   of Hemming's line,
grandson of Garmund   and great in battle.

XXVIII

Ongentheow, a Swedish king, comes up later, notably in the messenger's
speech to the Géat warriors (XL, XLI). He killed Haethcyn, brother
of Hygelac, who ordered a revenge attack (with the fatal blow admin-
istered by Eofer). Froda, king of the Heathobards, was killed fighting
against the Danes.

Freawaru, the name indicating a noble quality, may be a courtesy
title for Hrothgar's daughter.

1963–2040

The brave one went up   with his band of companions
along the sand,   treading the sea's edge
on the wide shore.   The world's candle shone,
the eager sun from the south.   Their sailing over,
they made swift headway   to where they had heard
the land's defender,   the war-fierce young king,
the slayer of Ongentheow   was sharing out treasure

within the stronghold.   At once Hygelac
was made aware of   Beowulf's arrival,
that there in the precincts   the protector of warriors
and shield-companions   had come safe and well,
unharmed from war-play,   to the court's hall.
The king requested   that room within quickly
should be made fit   for the guests on foot.
   The one who had survived   the ordeal safely
sat across from the other,   kinsman to kinsman,
when the lord of men   had greeted the loyal one
in due solemn speech.   Haereth's daughter
made the rounds of the hall   with beakers of mead;
kindly she pressed   the cups of strong drink
into the hands   of the heroes. Hygelac
courteously started   to question his comrade
in the noble hall.   He longed to know
all the Sea-Géats   had undergone.
   "Speak, dear Beowulf,   of what you bore
on your far travels,   after you fixed
so soon on an errand   across the salt sea,
a battle at Heorot!   Is Hrothgar's hardship,
the crisis facing   the famous king,
the better for you?   My breast was seething
in sorrow's storm;   I had no sure faith
in my dear man's mission.   Many times I begged you
to go nowhere near   the gory demon,
but to let the South-Danes   deal with the fight
with Grendel themselves.   I give thanks to God,
now that I see you   safe and sound!"
   The son of Ecgtheow,   Beowulf, spoke:
"Lord Hygelac,   many have heard of
a clash that is now   in no way a secret,
the battle there was   between me and Grendel,
in the very place   he brought to pass

73

a host of sorrows   on the warlike Scyldings,
a grief unending.   All that I avenged;
and so no kin   of Grendel's can ever
make proud claims   of a clamour at twilight,
not the longest-lived   of that loathsome race,
sunk in evil.   I set out at once,
up to the ring-hall   to hail Hrothgar;
and once aware   of my intent,
the celebrated   son of Healfdene
offered me a seat   beside his sons.
The gathering was glad: so great a mead-joy
of men at their seats   I have not seen
under heaven's arch.   The illustrious queen,
the land's bond of peace,   passed through the hall,
heartening the young men.   Often she handed one
a twisted ring   and re-took her seat.
At times Hrothgar's daughter   went up and down
offering the older men   the ale-bowl;
it was then I heard her   hailed as Freawaru
from the hall-benches,   as she gave heroes
the precious studded cup.   She is promised,
a gold-bedecked maiden,   to Froda's brave son.
The Scyldings' ruler   and protector of the realm
has managed it so;   for to settle a mass
of murderous quarrels   by means of the lady,
he reckons good counsel.   But rarely anywhere,
for some little time   when a prince is laid low,
is the war-spear idle,   though the bride be of worth!
    "It may test the patience   of the Heathobard prince
as with his lady   he enters the hall,
and that of each noble   of his nation,
to see Danish troops   treated with honour.
The ring-ornamented   heirlooms of old ones
will shine bright on them,   Heathobard belongings

74

when they were able   to wield their weapons,
till they led to disaster   their dear companions
in the war-play of shields,   and their own lives as well.

XXIX

*Withergyld is a renowned Heathobard warrior. One assumes Beowulf's
prescient comments as to the patching-up of a feud by an arranged
marriage are a poet's pointer to his qualities as a future candidate for
kingship, now he is back in his own land. (See the preliminary note to
I. The legend has it that Heorot is burnt to the ground in a later attack
by Ingeld, Froda's son and Freawaru's husband.) The listener or reader
is reminded of a tragic echo carried by a number of the events surrounding
those of the poem.*

Hondscio the Géat's death is described in XI.

2041–2100

"An old ash-spear warrior   will speak over the beer
as he spies a rich sword –   his mood will be savage,
remembering all   the battle-slaughter of men.
In his dark thoughts   he will try out the daring
of a young hero   with his heart's musings,
awakening the evil   of war with his words:
    'My friend, do you see   your father's sword,
the costly blade   that he bore with him
to the fray to the end,   till the final time
he donned the war-mask,   and the Danes slew him,
and those bold Scyldings   held the battle-field
when Withergyld had fallen,   and our finest with him?
And here is the boy   of one of these butchers
entering the hall –   he exults in his weapons,
he boasts of killing –   he carries the treasure
that by all rights   you ought to own!'
So he provokes   with painful reminders

75

on every occasion,   till the time comes
that a lady's warrior   sleeps laced with gore
from a blade's deep cut   for his father's deeds.
His life is forfeit.   The other has fled;
he knows the land well   and is clear away.
So on both sides   it will be broken,
the sworn oath of men   when deadly enmity
wells up in Ingeld,   and his love for his wife,
Freawaru, grows less   in surgings of grief.
I have no trust   in a truce with the Heathobards,
in a treaty that does not   trick the Danes,
in that bond of friendship.

"But I shall go back
to speaking of Grendel,   and soon you will see,
giver of fortunes,   how two foes fared
in hand-to-hand battle.   After heaven's gem
had slipped from the earth,   the angry monster,
night's menace and terror,   came to meet us,
as we watched unharmed   over the hall.
Hondscio's fateful   doom was at hand,
a wicked assault.   At once he fell,
the girded fighter,   as Grendel became
the mouth-slayer of   the famous young man;
he devoured all the body   of the dear warrior.
Yet none the sooner   meant the slayer
of terrible intent   and bloody tooth
to leave the gold-hall   empty-handed;
but mighty in strength   he made trial of me
with quick-grabbing claw.   His clutching troll-glove
was wide and wondrous,   with clasps of skilled working;
it was all fashioned   with fine cunning
from dragon-skin   by the devil's art.
The agent of awful   deeds intended
to pin me in it   in my innocence,

with many another.   He could not manage it,
as in anger   I sprang upright.
Too long in the telling   is the tale of my payment
to the country's enemy   for all his evil.
There, my prince,   I honoured your people
with my actions.   He escaped,
enjoyed life's pleasures   a little longer;
but his strong right hand   remained behind
at Heorot. Sadly   he slunk off out;
and his body sank   to the bottom of a lake.

XXX

Beowulf continues the account.

2101–2143

"For the fatal struggle   the Scyldings' lord-friend
rewarded me   with many rich treasures
of plated gold,   when we took our places
at the feast-table   the following day.
There was laughter and song.   An aged Scylding,
who had heard tell of much,   re-told old tales;
at times a brave warrior   addressed the glad-wood,
the harp with delight;   or someone held forth
in a song true and sad;   or else a strange legend
the full-hearted king   faithfully told.
At times, bent with age,   a battle-hero
took up a lament   for the loss of his youth,
his strength in the field.   His heart surged deep,
old and wise in his winters.   Much entered his mind.
    "So in that place   we took our pleasure
all day long   till night arrived
again among men.   Grendel's mother
was all too soon ready   to avenge her son

whom the war-hate of Weders   had done away with.
Filled with bitterness   the foul female came on
and exacted revenge: eagerly she slew
a noble there;   so now from Aeschere,
a wise and true counsellor,   the life was withdrawn.
Nor could they   as morning came,
the people of the Danes,   lay on a pyre
the death-wearied body   of the dear man
for the flame's burning.   She had borne it away
in her devil's embrace   to below the hill-stream.
That was for Hrothgar   the hardest sorrow
of all that had long   beset the lord.
The king implored me   with anguish at heart,
upon your life,   to risk losing mine
in the press of waters,   in a deed of prowess
and glorious renown: and he promised reward.
It is known far and wide   that I found the warden
of the flood's depths;   she was fierce and terrible.
For a time we two   attacked hand-to-hand;
the water boiled with blood;   in the battle-chamber
with a mighty sword   I struck off the head
of Grendel's mother.   By no means easily
did I escape death;   nor was I yet doomed;
and Healfdene's son,   the saviour of his race,
rewarded me   with many riches.

XXXI

The passing-on of Hrothgar's gifts to his king and queen ends Beowulf's Danish venture; and with his own fifty-year rule referred to in the briefest of terms, the stage is set for a feat of old age. (There is also an interesting reference to what seems to be a period of adolescent immaturity on his part.)

Hereric's nephew is Heardred.

"The people's king   kept honourable custom;   2144–2220
in no way was I   to lose my award,
the prize of prowess.   He proffered treasures,
Healfdene's son,   of my heart's choosing.
These, noble king,   will be carried to you;
gladly I offer them.   All my happiness
is fixed in you: few kin do I have
whom I hold close,   but only you, Hygelac!"
    A boar's-head banner   he bid be brought in,
a battle-steep helmet,   a steel-grey breastplate,
an adorned war-sword,   and uttered these words:
    "The wise prince Hrothgar   awarded me
this raiment of war;   and said that at once
I should inform you   of where it was from.
He said for a long time   the Scyldings' leader,
king Heorogar   had hold of it.
Yet he did not hand on   to his own son,
the worthy Heoroweard,   loyal as he was,
this war-apparel.   Enjoy it all well!"
    I heard that four horses   came following the armour,
all alike, swift   and apple-yellow.
Into the keeping   of the king
went horses and treasure: a true kinsman's deed!
No-one should knit   a net of malice
in dark cunning,   or plot secret death
for a close companion.   To the king his uncle,
the hardy in battle,   Beowulf was loyal;
and each took to heart   the other's happiness.
    I heard that he offered   the neck-band to Hygd,
the wondrous ornament   the princess Wealhtheow
had handed him;   and three horses too,
supple and saddle-bright.   When Hygd accepted
the necklace, from that day   her breast was ennobled.

So Ecgtheow's son   showed true courage,
a renowned warrior,   noble in action,
sound in judgement.   No drunken sot striking
his hearth-companions,   no uncouth lout he:
but brave in battle,   in the broad range
of his gifts from God,   with the greatest art
a man has, he lived.   For a long time
he was thought little of,   looked on with scorn
by the men of the Géats;   nor at the mead-bench
was he held in great worth   by the lord of the Weders.
It was strongly felt   that he was slothful,
a man of no vigour.   A reversal came
to these shaming thoughts   in his shining fame.

    The battle-brave prince,   protector of men,
bid Hrethel's heirloom   be brought in,
a gold-adorned sword;   in the Géats at that time
there was nothing more precious   of that nature.
This now he laid   in Beowulf's lap;
and gave him seven thousand   hides of ground
with a grand throne-hall.   Each now held
land in the country,   a castle-dwelling
with ancestral rights;   but the larger was owned
by the more illustrious,   a king's estate.

    In later days   when Hygelac was laid low
in the crash of battle,   it came to pass,
after battle-blades   had been the slayer
of Heardred his son   past his shield-cover,
when the warlike Scylfings,   hard grim warriors,
caught up with him   in his victorious kingdom,
and heavily attacked   Hereric's nephew –
it was after this   that the broad ample realm
was given to Beowulf.   The new king governed
for fifty winters.   Wisely and well
he ruled in his age –   until the rise

in the dark of night   of a dragon's tyranny.
In its high lair   it watched over a hoard
in a barrow of steep stone.   Down below
lay a secret passage.   Some person or other
followed it through   and found himself
by the heathen treasure,   where his hand picked up
a jewelled cup.   Later the creature
saw a thief's skill   had tricked it while sleeping.
This was the reason   its anger arose,
and those living near   learnt of its rage.

XXXII
We learn more of the hoard's history later (XLI, XLII).

The man who set off   the serpent's anguish   2221–2311
in no way had planned   to plunder its hoard.
He was the serf   of a hero's son,
in trouble for a crime   he had committed.
In dire hardship,   flying blows of hatred,
in search of shelter   he stumbled in there.
As he looked round   at what lay inside
at once pure horror   possessed the stranger;
from the ghastly shape   he stole away,
catching up as he went   a precious cup
in the perilous moment.   There were many such there,
ancient treasures   in the earth-house,
for in times past   a certain person
had taken thought   and hidden there
the towering legacy   of a noble tribe,
its dearest fortune.   Death took all
of that early time;   and an old warrior
who had survived   awaited the same,
the last left, mourning   the loss of friends.

Only a short time   might he savour
the riches of the past.   A barrow stood ready
near the sea's waves,   newly made
and hard of access   on a headland.
The keeper of the rings   carried inside it
the plated gold,   a great and grand fortune
in need of safe store.   He made a short speech:
    "Earth, now hold   what heroes could not,
the wealth of nobles!   Look how men won it
from you of old!   The awful ravage
of war has driven   to their death
all my people;   and each who died
knew joy in hall.   I have none to hold
the sword, or to clean   the plated cup,
the precious goblet.   The old people are gone.
The hard, gold-adorned   helmet of war
will lose its plating;   the polishers sleep
who should burnish   the battle-masks;
the coat-of-mail   that in the armed clash,
the breaking of shields,   bore the sword's bite,
decays like its owner.   Nor can the ringed corselet
range far and wide   with the war-leader
in the ranks of heroes.   The harp's joy is gone,
the glad-wood's delighting.   Nor does the good hawk
skim through the hall,   nor does the swift horse
stamp in the courtyard.   Cruel death
has exiled many   of the race of men!"
    Mournful and alone   he made his lament,
the last survivor,   and paced about sadly
night and day   until death's wave
touched his heart.   The open hoard
was lit upon   by the twilight-attacker,
the burning one   that seeks out barrows,
the malicious bare dragon   that flies in the dark,

wrapped in fire,   mightily feared
by dwellers on earth.   It likes to discover
a hoard in the ground   and guard heathen gold,
an ancient sentinel,   availing nothing.
    The enemy of the people   lay at the place
of the hoard in the earth   for three hundred years,
supreme in its power,   until a person
aroused its rage.   He robbed it of a goblet
of plated gold   to give his liege lord
and beg for forgiveness.   The store was broken into,
the stack of treasure less;   and the destitute man
had his prayer allowed.   His liege lord looked at
the work of hands far back   for the first time.
    When the serpent awoke   its anger was kindled;
hurrying over the rock   with war in its heart,
it saw the foe's footprints   where he had stepped up
deftly in secret   by the dragon's head.
So an undoomed man   may lightly endure
the cares of an outcast,   if he hold close to
the Ruler's good grace.   The hoard-guardian searched
along the ground eagerly   after the being
that had insulted it   in its sleep.
Hot and wrathful   it prowled round the mound
again and again;   there was no-one outside
in that waste place.   It relished its war-thoughts,
its blood-lust. At times   going back in the cave
it sought the rich cup;   but soon it was sure
that someone or other   had stumbled on the gold,
its wealth of treasure.   The barrow-warden
restlessly waited   till dusk arrived.
The hoard's sentinel   seethed with rage;
the foul thing was ready   to repay with flame
the rich goblet's theft.   The daylight was going;
in its longing for darkness   it did not linger

on the barrow wall   but went forth in flame,
furnished with fire.   The first time was as awful
for the people in the land   as the last was to be
in its swiftness and grief   for their treasure-giver.

XXXIII

*The Hetware were a tribe on the lower Rhine associated with the
Frisians. The thirty pieces of armour Beowulf swims back with are from
the corpses of their soldiers. Hygelac's son Heardred is slain by the
mighty Swedish king Onela (mentioned in I as Hrothgar's brother-
in-law).*

The creature began   to belch out flame,   2312–2390
to burn the bright houses;   the people were horrified
at the fire's flare;   the hateful air-flier
meant to leave nothing   there alive.
The serpent's warfare   was seen far and near,
the ruin wrought   by the rancorous foe,
the enemy's hate,   its humbling of
the Géat race.   Before the sun rose
it rushed back to its hoard,   its rich hidden hall.
It had ringed the folk   of the land with fire,
a burning flame.   It trusted in battle
and its barrow's high wall: its hopes deceived it.
   Quickly to Beowulf   the dire news was brought
that his own home,   the most handsome of buildings,
the gift-seat of the Géats,   was burnt to the ground
in swathes of flame.   A sorrow of the heart
it was to the good man,   a great grief of mind.
The king supposed   he had sorely angered
the eternal Lord,   the Ruler of all,
broken old law.   Thoughts dark and low
welled up, far   from his usual way.

The fire-dragon   had charred with flame
the land by the sea   and its safe stronghold,
the nation's bulwark.   Vengeance-bent
was the war-chief now,   the Weder king.
The warriors' protector,   prince of nobles,
ordered to be made   out of iron
a wondrous shield;   he knew all too well
a shield of forest-wood   was no safeguard,
timber in the flame.   The finest of princes
was fated to meet   the last of his fleeting
days in the world,   and the dragon as well,
though it had held   the hoard for so long.
    The ring-lord scorned   to go and seek out
the far-flier with   a full force of men,
an army. Fearless   of the fray,
he set no store   on the serpent's power,
its strength or boldness.   He had survived
many onslaughts,   adventures of hardship,
crashes of battle,   a man blessed with victory
long after cleansing   the Danish king's hall,
and finally crushing   Grendel's family
of hated race.
                In hand-to-hand conflicts
not the least was it   when Hygelac was lost,
the country's loved lord   and Géat king,
the son of Hrethel,   the sword drinking his blood,
when in Friesland   he was felled by the blade
in the rush of battle.   From there Beowulf came,
by his strength surviving   a feat of swimming;
thirty pieces of armour   he carried on his arm,
he alone,   as he entered the wave.
No reason was there   for the Hetware to rejoice
in the foot-battle   when they bore their shields
forward against him;   few returned

from the hardy warrior   to reach their homes.
Then Ecgtheow's son   swam the water's expanse,
oppressed, all-alone.   Arriving back home
he was offered by Hygd   a hoard of ringed treasures,
a king's seat, a country.   She was unsure
if her son could hold   the sovereign throne
against an outsider,   with Hygelac gone.
The bereaved nation   none the sooner
found a way   to make the warrior
accept a higher   rank than Heardred
and consent   to be their king;
but honourably Beowulf   backed the boy
with good advice,   till he grew old enough
to rule the Géats.   Heardred gave haven
to the sons of Ohthere   from over the sea;
the exiles had risen   against their ruler,
their kinsman Onela,   the mightiest of sea-kings
that in Sweden   shared out treasure,
the famed Scylfing prince.   So Heardred fell.
For his offer of succour   the son of Hygelac
took a mortal blow   from a brandished sword.
Ongentheow's son,   Onela, departed,
took himself home,   after Heardred had fallen.
It was now open   for Beowulf to ascend
the throne of the Géats.   A good king was he!

XXXIV

The accidental manslaughter of brother by brother was punishable; but the father Hrethel could not lift his hand against his son. As with reminders of old feuding, an elegiac moment seems to have its natural place in Anglo-Saxon epic (of which Beowulf *is our one example), providing colour for the action, rather than at once proceeding with it.*

For his leader's death   he made sure later   2391–2459
to exact payment;   to destitute Eadgils
he was an ally,   and sent out an army
of warriors and weapons   across the wide sea
to Ohthere's son.   On a sad grim journey
Eadgils slew Onela   and so took revenge.
  The son of Ecgtheow   had survived
bitter clashes   and bold rebellions,
each dire attack,   until the day
that he must settle   with the serpent.
With eleven others   the lord of the Géats
went in fury   to face the dragon.
He had learnt the cause   of the evil crisis
hanging over his people;   for he was handed
the famed precious cup   by the one who found it.
The man who had set   all that strife in motion
became the thirteenth   of the band,
a wretched captive,   now compelled
to point out the way.   He went against his will
to where he had seen   a certain earth-chamber,
a cave in the ground   lying close to the sea,
the waves' surge and tumult,   and stacked high inside
with twisted gold ornaments.   The awful sentinel,
the underground ancient,   all-eager for battle,
guarded the riches.   Going in there
was no easy bargain   for any man.
  The battle-brave king   sat down on the cliff,
the gold-friend of Géats,   and gave his blessing
to his hearth-companions.   He was sad at heart,
restless, death-ready,   the destiny near
past measure that came   to meet the old man,
to seek out the soul's   hoard of riches, to sunder
life from body.   Now not for long
was his being to be   wound about in flesh.

87

Beowulf spoke,   son of Ecgtheow:
"In my youth I survived   many onslaughts of war,
high moments of battle.   I remember it all.
Seven winters was I   when the people's sovereign,
their ring-lord and friend,   took me from my father.
I was in the keeping   of Hrethel the king,
who rewarded our kinship   with riches and feasting.
In his life he was never   less fond of me,
a warrior in his stronghold,   than of his sons,
Herebeald or Haethcyn   or my dear Hygelac.
For the eldest   by grim accident
on his brother's part   a death-bed was prepared.
Haethcyn felled   his friend and lord,
when an arrow   aimed from his horn-bow,
wide of its target,   took Herebeald's life,
a bloody shaft   from brother to brother.
That was a crime   without compensation,
a terrible attack,   awful, heart-wearying;
yet the prince was fated   to fall unavenged.
   "So too an old man   suffers an anguish
that cannot be eased   when his condemned son
rides young on the gallows.   A song of grief
may he then sing,   as his son hangs
at the raven's pleasure,   and he has no power,
old and wise as he is,   to assist him at all.
Always he is reminded,   every morning,
of his son's way elsewhere.   To wait for another
son and heir   within the stronghold
he has no heart,   now the first one has had
his fill of deeds   in the harsh need of death.
Sorrowful he sees   in his son's dwelling
the wine-hall deserted,   now the wind's home,
bereft of joy;   the brave horsemen sleep
hidden in the grave;   the harp's sound is gone;
no games fill the courtyards   as they did long ago.

XXXV

Beowulf continues to dwell on the events leading up to his kingship. It is as though all his service as king is to be summed up in his final act. The Swedes are a tribe to the north of the Géats.

"He lies on his couch,   he chants a sad lay,   2460–2601
the one left for the one gone;   it is all too large,
the great rooms, the fields.   So the guardian of the Géats
held in his heart   for Herebeald
a swelling sorrow.   For the assault
he was powerless to make   the slayer pay.
He could not take up arms   any the sooner
against the lord Haethcyn   though loving him not.
Then with despair   lying deep in him
Hrethel lost earthly joy   and gained God's light.
He left his sons   the estate they were due,
his land and townships   when he quit life.
    "A bitter quarrel broke out   between Swedes and Géats
across the wide waters,   each accusing the other;
harsh fighting took place   after Hrethel died.
The sons of Ongentheow   were battle-strong, brave;
they had no interest   in upholding a truce
beyond the shores;   but around Hreosnaburg
often waged war   with awful slaughter.
My dear kinsmen   dealt revenge
for the wicked attacks,   as is well-known;
though one of them lost   his life in payment,
a hard bargain.   For to Haethcyn,
the prince of the Géats,   the battle proved fatal.
In the morning, I heard,   his brother Hygelac
had revenge on the slayer   by the sword's edge.
When Ongentheow   challenged Eofor,
the old Scylfing sank down,   by a sword-thrust made pale;
his helmet had split.   Eofer's hand, knowing
the blood-feud well,   did not spare the death-blow.

"Hygelac the king   accorded me riches,
and I paid on the battlefield   as it befell me
with the bright sword.   He bestowed on me land,
an ancestral home.   He had no need at all
to look out for   a lesser warrior,
among the Gar-Danes   or the Gifthas
or in Sweden,   to sell his hire.
In front of him always   on foot in the field
I took the lead station;   and so shall I still
engage in the fray,   while this sword endures
that early or late   often has served me,
since in my prowess   I slew Daeghrefn,
champion of the Hugas,   by my hand's strength.
He failed to bear   the bodies' trappings,
the prize-armour up to   the Frisian prince;
for he fell in combat,   keeper of the banner,
noble in courage.   Nor did the sword slay him:
my battle-grip   broke up his bone-house,
laid siege to his heart.   Now shall this hand
and this hard blade   do battle for the hoard."
    With proud words Beowulf   pledged himself
a final time.   "Many risks in fighting
were mine in my youth;   yet shall I still,
the land's old protector,   press forward to peril
with a deed of renown –   if the evil ravager
will leave his cave   to come my way!"
Then he addressed   each dear warrior,
his close companions   and keen shield-carriers,
for the very last time.   "I would not take a sword,
go armed at the serpent,   if I saw how else
to face the monster   and fulfil my pledge –
to come to grips differently,   as against Grendel.
I expect to feel   the hot fire of battle,
its poisonous breath;   which is why I bear

a breastplate and shield.   I shall not flee a footstep
from the mound-warden,   but there at the wall
we will face it out   as Fate will have it,
the Master of all.   My mind is made up:
fine words are not needed   against the fierce-flier!
Wait on the barrow   behind your breastplates,
warriors in war-gear,   and see which one of us
in the savage assault   with all its injury
lasts the better.   It is not your burden.
No man other   than myself
need use his might   against the monster
in an act of valour.   By my warrior's virtue
I shall win gold,   or else the grim fray,
the dread loss of life   will take off your lord!"
    The renowned champion   rose with his shield,
stern in his helmet   and corslet-harness;
and sure in his one man's   might alone,
moved on down the cliff: no coward's venture!
    He saw by the wall,   the warrior foremost
in noble virtue,   veteran of many
crashes of war   and clashes of foot-troops,
a stone arch standing,   and a stream-of-fire
that broke from the barrow.   A blazing surge
was that battle-current;   he could not but be burnt
if he were to stay there   the slightest time,
down by the hoard   in the dragon's flame.
In an angry passion   the Géat prince
let a shout burst out   from his breast,
a fierce roar.   Ringing battle-clear
the sound went in   under the grey stone.
Hate was awoken.   The hoard-minder knew
the voice of man;   the time had vanished
for a truce to be sought.   Straightaway
the monster's breath   boiled through the rock,

the hot steam of battle,   and the ground boomed.
The warrior at the mound,   the lord of the Weders,
swung up his shield   at the strange awful thing;
the crouched being's heart   was all caught up
in battle-lust.   The brave war-king
had his sword out,   the sharpest of blades,
an old heirloom.   Each combatant,
intent on harm,   had a horror of the other.
Unflinching he stood,   the lord-friend of men,
behind his high shield;   as the serpent speedily
coiled itself up,   the armed one awaited.
It came out burning,   streaming bow-bent,
flying to its fate.   The shield defended
life and limb   for not as long
as the famed king   had hoped for before.
There on that day   fate denied him
for the first time   the final outcome
of battle-glory.   The prince raised the great
ancestral sword   and struck at the glittering
terrible form;   but the edge failed,
bright against the bone,   biting less sharply
than the people's king   in his desperate case
had high need of.   The hoard-protector
in savage anger   at the battle-stroke
threw slaughterous fire;   the flame-light of war
leapt far and wide.   The gold-friend of the Géats
boasted no victory;   the blade-of-war failed,
unsheathed in the fray,   as it should not have done,
the splendid old iron-edge.   It was no easy journey
for the celebrated   son of Ecgtheow
to abandon the surface   of the earth.
Elsewhere he must   take up his abode
against his will,   as all shall depart
the fleeting day.   It was not long before

the fearsome creatures   clashed again.
The guardian of the hoard   took fresh heart;
its breast pulsed with breath,   with the other at peril
of the flame's clutch and clasp   who had been king.
Not at all   did the sons of nobles,
his fellow-warriors,   form a group round him
as was fitting;   but they fled to the forest
to hold on to life.   In the heart of one
sorrow surged.   None of true sense
can ever discard   a claim of kinship.

XXXVI

*Wiglaf's father fought on Onela's side against the Swedish exiles who
sought sanctuary at the Géatish court; yet Wiglaf in his allegiance is
a true Géat. He, his father and Beowulf all belong to the Waegmunding
family (XXXVIII). The inter-tribal and family linkage is not
entirely clear but a deeper bond is, that seems virtually to transform a
'claim of kinship' to the debt of a fellow-human.*

He was called Wiglaf,   son of Weohstan,   2602–2693
prince of the Scylfings,   a prized shield-warrior,
kinsman of Aelfhere.   He saw his overlord
in his war-helmet   in extremes from the heat.
He looked back at the favours   his lord had allowed him,
the wealthy dwelling-place   of the Waegmundings,
the land-rights all   as his father had owned them;
and he could not hold back.   His hand seized the shield,
the yellow linden buckler,   and he drew the old blade
known among men   to have been owned by Eanmund,
Ohthere's son.   By Weohstan's sword
he had fallen in the fray,   a friendless exile;
and the slayer had carried   to Eanmund's kinsmen
the ringed breastplate,   the bright-gleaming helmet,

the old blade made by giants.   Onela awarded him
the instruments of war,   fit for fine action,
of his family kinsman.   He did not speak of the feud,
though the other had slain   the son of his brother.
For many half-years   Weohstan held
the adorned battle-treasures,   the sword and breastplate,
for the son to bear   with the father's bravery;
and he gave to Wiglaf   in the presence of the Géats
a great heap of armour,   when old, at life's end,
he went on his way.   Now was the first time
the fledgling warrior   was to follow
his beloved ruler   in the rush of battle.
His courage did not melt;   and his kinsman's heirloom
did not fail in the fray.   The serpent found that out
after they met   in battle-encounter.
Sad at heart   Wiglaf spoke
many true words   to the men about him:
    "I remember the time   when we drank mead,
and in the ale-hall   undertook
to repay our lord   for all our riches –
our battle-harness,   our helmets, hard swords.
If his need was ever   as it is now
we promised him this.   And the king picked us
of his own will   out of the army
for the adventure,   valuing us
worthy of glory.   He gave me these treasures,
and held us all   as brave helmet-wearers;
though he intended   alone to accomplish
the valiant deed,   defending his people.
He has carried out   acts of courage
above all men.   The day has arrived
when our sovereign lord   needs the support
of good men of the field.   Let us go forward
and help the war-leader   as long as it lasts,

the fierce fire-terror!   God knows for myself
I would be far happier   for the flame to lap
my body's shell   with my gold-sharer.
To me it seems base   to bear our shields
away back home,   without going to battle
to fell the foe,   and defend the life
of the prince of the Weders.   I know well
he does not deserve   to endure this alone,
in the Géat army   alone to suffer
and sink in the fight.   Let our swords and helmets,
battle-gear, breastplates   be held in common!"
   Then through the death-haze   he went in his helmet
to stand by his lord,   and spoke a few words:
"Dear Beowulf,   do everything well.
Just as you said   in your youth long ago,
that as long as you lived   you would never allow
your name to fade,   so now, prince famed
for your deeds, single-minded,   use all your might
to save your life.   I will support you!"
   After he spoke   the serpent in fury
emerged again,   a foul evil thing
shining in fire-streams,   and set on its foes,
the enemy men.   The shield burned up
to the boss in a flame-swirl;   nor could the breastplate
be of much use   to the youthful warrior;
but bold and alert   he moved in behind
his kinsman's shield   when his own was consumed
entirely by fire.   Mindful of his fame
was the battle-king,   who in brute force
struck with the war-sword   with such grim strength
that it stood in the head.   But Naegling shattered,
Beowulf's blade,   it failed in the battle,
grey-coloured, old.   It was not granted him
to wield to advantage   a battle-edge of iron

in the fray. His hand,   as I have heard,
was so very strong   that in the stroke
he overtaxed each sword.   To arm himself
with a war-blooded blade   had served him no better.
   For a third time   the terrible fire-dragon,
the enemy of the land   intent on destruction,
now seeing its chance,   charged at the famous one;
hot and battle-fierce   it seized the whole neck
in its sharp fangs.   Beowulf was splashed
with his life-blood   that welled up in a wave.

XXXVII

The third epic feat is completed, by a hero all too human.
   There is a simplicity and a brevity about the concluding events of the
poem (not including the messenger's speech of XL, XLI), that Beowulf's
last speeches seem to introduce.

To aid the king   in his hour of need   2694–2751
I heard the man near him   showed high valour,
a nerve and skill   that were natural to him.
He did not aim at the head,   but the hand burned
of the hero who brought   help to his kinsman,
as he lunged at the foe   a little lower.
The sword of the armed one,   shining gold-plated,
dived in – and the fire   began to die down
after that gash.   Gathering his senses
the king himself drew   a deadly battle-knife,
cruelly sharp,   that he wore on his corslet;
and the guardian of men   sliced the serpent in the middle.
The enemy was downed,   laid low by daring –
the noble kinsmen   had killed it there,
the two together.   At a time of need
so should a man act! –

                    For the mighty one
the victory-deed   was the last of his doing,
his work in the world.   The wound began
to burn and swell   he had suffered before
from the earth-dragon.   Too soon he discovered
the venom welling   with deadly violence
within his breast.   Over to the wall
the chieftain went,   wise, knowing in thought,
for a place to sit down.   He saw the work of giants,
how the earth-house   held inside it
a vault of stone   secured by pillars.
Then with his hands   the worthiest of henchmen
washed his lord   and friend with water,
the prince of great fame,   gory with battle,
weary with fighting,   and unfastened his helmet.
   Beowulf spoke   in spite of his injuries,
his mortal wound.   He knew well
he had endured   his span of days,
earthly joys.   It was over and gone,
the sum of living.   Death loomed all-near.
"My garments of war   I would have wished now
to give to my son,   if I had been granted
an heir to look after   all that I leave,
my body's trappings.   I ruled the tribe
for fifty winters.   No chieftain came forth
from neighbouring peoples   to press me in battle,
to take up the sword   and threaten with terror,
approach with an army.   At home I awaited
what time held in store,   kept well what I had;
and I sought no cunning   conflict, nor swore
a pack of false oaths.   I find joy in all this,
weak as I am   from mortal wounds.
The Ruler of men   has no need to reproach me
with the slaying of kin,   as the time comes for life

to quit my body.   Go you now quickly
and search out the hoard   beneath the grey stone,
beloved Wiglaf.   The serpent lies still,
it sleeps sore-wounded,   away from its riches.
Fast about it: my eyes would feast
on the wealth of times gone,   the treasures of gold,
the bright jewelled ornaments.   So the more gently
for seeing the fortune,   I can forgo all,
my life and my land   that I have held long."

XXXVIII

The treasure-hoard has its own character and mystery within the story.

I heard that at once,   after these words,   2752–2820
the son of Weohstan   obeyed the wounded
war-weakened lord.   In linked corslet he went,
his ringed coat-of-mail,   beneath the mound's roof.
Past where the king sat   the keen young warrior,
in victory proud,   saw a precious heap
of jewels and gold   glittering on the ground,
with works of wonder   on the walls.
In the lair of the serpent,   the old twilight-flier,
he saw beakers of past men,   ornamental bowls
with no polisher by,   and pieces fallen away.
Many helmets lay round,   rusty and ancient,
and a mass of bracelets   most cunningly made.
Treasure can easily   overcome anyone,
a deep hoard of gold.   Let him hide it who will!
   And he saw hanging   high over the riches
an all-golden banner,   greatest of marvels,
woven by hands' craft.   A light came off it
that let him see   the surface of the ground.
He gazed at the treasure.   There was no trace

of the serpent there,   for the sword had dispatched it.
I heard the barrow,   built by old giants,
was plundered now   by one person alone.
He gathered in his bosom   goblets and plates
at will, and he took   the banner as well,
brightest of beacons.   The sharp iron blade
of the old prince's weapon   earlier had wounded
the long-time guard   of the mound's great treasures.
With a hot fire of terror,   a fierce flame
death-streaming out   into the dark,
it defended the hoard,   till the fatal blow.
Eager to return,   urged on by the riches,
the king's man made haste.   A hunger broke out
in the brave youth to know   if he might yet see
the lord of the Weders,   all-weakened in power,
alive in the place   where he had left him.
Carrying the riches   to his king
he found him bleeding,   the famous prince
at life's end.   Again he began
to splash him with water,   till speech started
to break from the storehouse   of his heart.
The old man spoke to the young,   seeing the gold:
    "In words I give thanks   to the King of Glory,
the Eternal Lord,   the Ruler of All,
for the great fortune   I gaze on here,
that I could win   wealth such as this
before my death-day   for my people.
Now I have sold   my old life-span
for this rich store,   do you stay and attend to
the nation's need!   I can be here no more.
Bid my fine warriors,   after my burning,
make ready a handsome   mound at the headland.
At Hronesness   it shall tower high
as a reminder   to my people,

and seafarers later   shall speak of it
as Beowulf's Hill,   when in their boats
they drive from afar   on the dark of the flood."
   The brave-minded king   freed the gold collar
from his neck, and gave it   to his follower,
with his breastplate and ring   and gold-rich helmet,
and bid the young warrior   use them well.
"You live on,   the last of our family
of the Waegmundings.   My worthy kinsmen
have left to follow   the lure of fate,
to endure its end.   I must after them."
   The old man uttered   the thoughts of his mind
no more before   his body chose
the battle-heat of the pyre.   His soul departed
his breast, to seek judgement   upon the just.

XXXIX

*Up to the final tableau of young man and old, the Wiglaf episode
recalls, as if from a long way off, something of the tie of closeness between
Beowulf and Hrothgar; an echo that in a nameless way is absorbed into
the tragic depth.*

It went very hard   with the young warrior,   2821–2891
as he looked at   his dearest lord
upon the ground   in grievous state
at life's end.   The killer lay too,
the dire earth-dragon   in its own destruction,
banished from being.   No more was the barrow-hoard
in the control   of the cruelly-coiled serpent;
for hard iron blades,   scarred in battle,
forged under the hammer,   had fetched it off.
So the far-flier   had fallen to the ground
by the store-chamber,   stilled by its wounds.

No more did it spin   and sport through the air,
making an appearance   at midnight, proud
of the treasure it owned.   It had been toppled
to earth by the hand's work   of the war-hero.
In truth not many   men of the land,
as I have heard,   however strong,
and though they were daring   in every deed,
had ever braved   that venomous breath,
or disturbed the treasure-hall   with their hands,
once aware   of the guardian watching
at the mound-dwelling.   The mass of rich treasure
was paid for by Beowulf   with all his being.
Each of the two   had found the end
of fleeting life.   It was not long
till the battle-shirkers   abandoned the forest,
ten cowards who did not   keep their promise,
who had not dared   to dart their spears
when their noble lord   had direst need.
Now in shame   they carried their shields
and war-gear to where   the old one lay.
They looked at Wiglaf.   Wearily he sat,
the foot-warrior at   his lord-friend's shoulder,
trying to wake him   with water in vain.
Deep though he wished it,   he had no way
in the world to hold onto   life in the hero,
or alter anything   of the Almighty.
The judgement of God   governed each one
of the deeds of men,   as it does now.
  Easy to find   were the angry words
of the noble to those   whose nerve had gone.
Wiglaf looked at them   without love,
Weohstan's son,   sad at heart.

"Your liege lord   who let you keep
the costly troop-armour   that you carry,
who on the ale-bench   often presented,
a prince to his subjects   sitting in hall,
a helmet and breastplate   of the best quality
that he could find,   far or near –
any speaker   of truth will say
he utterly wasted   all that war-clothing,
even as one   under hard siege.
The people's king   had no cause to boast of
his battle-companions.   God so accorded,
the Victory-Lord,   that alone with the blade
he avenged himself,   when valour was scarce.
I could provide   little protection
to my kinsman's   life in the conflict;
yet I started to help him   beyond my strength.
When my sword struck   the slaughterous foe
it was ever weaker,   the fire-wave surged out
from its head with less force.   Too few defenders
surrounded the king   when his hour came.
Now the giving of swords,   the receiving of treasure,
all joy of inheritance,   of the loved home,
cease for your kind.   You and your kinsfolk
will wander and roam   with no right of land,
every last man,   when nobles learn
far and wide   about your flight,
that most shameful act.   For every man
death is better   than to live in disgrace."

XL

The messenger dwells on the feud between the Swedes and the Géats, to make clear the danger the latter are at once in, following the death of their king. There is a reference to Ongentheow's fate in XXVIII (see the preliminary note to that section).

He bid the battle-feat   be announced   2892–2945
at the camp high up   on the cliff, where a host
of noble shield-warriors   had sat, sad at heart,
all morning long,   with two things in mind,
the day of death   of the dear man
or his return.   The one who rode up
with the news to the headland   held back little,
but spoke the truth freely   in front of all.
   "The Weder people's   granter of wishes,
the Géat lord   lies still on his death-bed,
a dread resting-place,   the serpent's doing.
By him is the body,   sawn by the short blade,
of his mortal enemy.   He was unable
to wound the monster   in any way
by use of the sword.   Beside Beowulf
Wiglaf sits,   son of Weohstan,
the living man   by the unliving;
weary at heart   he holds watch by the head
of friend and foe.   A time of dire fighting
is to come for the people,   when the fall of the prince
is known afar,   and the news has reached
the Franks and the Frisians.   A grim feud began
with the Huga tribe   when Hygelac sailed
to the land of the Frisians   with a sea-force.
There the Hetware   met him in war,
and their greater power   soon brought it to pass
that our armoured leader   was overwhelmed
and sank in the troops: our lord shared no spoils
of war with the veterans.   Since then no warmth
has come our way   from the Merovingian king.
   "From the Swedish people   I do not expect
peace or good faith.   That Ongentheow
deprived Haethcyn,   the son of Hrethel,
of life by Ravenswood   is well known;

it was when the War-Scylfings   were first assailed
for their arrogance   by the Géat tribe.
At once the old fierce   father of Ohthere
gave a terrible   blow in return:
he killed the sea-prince   and set free his own wife,
the aged lady   who had lost her gold,
mother of Ohthere   and of Onela;
and then hunted down   his hated enemies,
who leaderless   and at no little cost
slipped away   into Ravenswood.
His men circled all   as yet spared by the sword,
the wounded and weary.   That woeful band
throughout the night   was threatened with misery.
He said, come morning,   some he would slay
with the sword's sharp edge;   some on the gallows
would swing for birds' sport.   Again the sad crew
drew comfort when   at break of day
they heard the song   of Hygelac's horn
sound with the trumpet.   The trusty prince
with a picked force   had found the track.

XLI

*We may assume the instructions as to the fate of the hoard come from
Wiglaf. But the messenger's words are invested with an uncanny
authority. There may be something ambivalent in his role, touching on
that of an ancient Greek chorus.*

"The gory trail   of Swedes and Géats   2946–3057
in murderous conflict   was all too clear,
where fighting men   had fostered the feud.
Ongentheow left   with his loyal band
to seek out a stronghold;   old and sad,
the revered leader   turned aside in retreat.

He had heard   of Hygelac's fighting,
his high battle-prowess,   and now had no hope
of rallying resistance   against the war-rovers
from over the water,   to keep safe his wealth
and wife and children.   Again the old man
ducked behind an earth-wall.   The Swedish warriors
were harried further.   Hygelac's banner
was raised all over   their place of refuge,
as Hrethel's people   pressed through the enclosure.
They hunted down Ongentheow   of the grey hair,
and brought him to bay   with their sharp blades.
The sovereign of the land   now had to submit
to Eofor's will.   Wulf, son of Wonred,
Eofor's brother,   struck out in anger,
and at the sword's blow   blood sprang from the veins
under Ongentheow's hair.   Still unafraid,
the aged Scylfing,   the people's king, swiftly
regained his poise   and gave in repayment
for the bloody challenge   a worse exchange.
The bold son of Wonred,   Wulf, was unable
to offer a counter-blow   as the old man
had hacked right through   the helmet on his head;
and stained with blood   he had to stoop
and fall on the ground –   though not as yet fated,
since he recovered   from the racking wound.
With his brother outstretched,   the brave Eofor,
Hygelac's follower,   forced his broad blade
down past the shield's barrier   to shatter the helmet –
both sword and helmet   the old skilled work of giants –
and the king and land's leader   lay mortally struck.
Then there were many   to bind up Wulf's wound,
at once bear him off,   now that the battle-field
clearly lay   under their control.
It fell to one warrior   to rifle the other;

so Eofor took   from Ongentheow
iron corslet and helmet   and hard hilted sword,
and carried to Hygelac   the old man's war-harness.
He took hold of the treasures,   and handsomely pledged
a public reward;   and kept his promise.
The lord of the Géats,   Hrethel's son, gave
to Eofor and Wulf,   when he arrived home,
a fine fortune   for their feats in battle.
Land and linked rings   worth a lakh of silver coins
he gave to each   for the glory they had won;
and no man on earth   need grudge the amount.
And his only daughter   he bestowed upon Eofor
as an earnest of friendship,   and to honour his home.
    "Because of this   bitter enmity,
these murderous assaults   of men, I expect
the Swedish people   will seek us out,
when they learn   our lord and leader
is parted from life.   It was he who protected
our land, our fortune,   our fighting men
from all our foes,   when the great ones had fallen.
He did well for his people.   In truth he performed
a hero's deeds.
                    "Now haste is best.
Let us look upon   our king where he lies,
who gave us our wealth,   and fetch him away
to the funeral fire.   All that is found
shall melt in flame   with the brave man.
A treasure-hoard lies   of untold gold,
fiercely bargained for,   bought at the last
with his very life.   The flames shall enfold it,
the fire unmake all.   No man in memory
may bear a bright token;   no beautiful maiden
may set on her neck   an adorning circlet;
but bare of all gold,   again and again

they shall tread sadly   in a strange land.
Now the war-leader   has laid aside laughter
and all good cheer.   Soon in chill hands
shall many a spear   be raised in the mornings,
held in the grasp.   No harp's sound shall stir
the men of battle;   but the black raven,
swift over the dead,   will say many things,
and tell the eagle   of its luck with the eating,
when it roved with the wolf   to rifle the slain."
    The valiant messenger   told the men
the wretched news.   Nor was he far wrong
in fact or foretelling.   The full troop rose,
going sadly under   Earnaness
with welling tears   to the terrible sight.
On the sand they found him.   His soul had left
and he lay at rest,   who had given them riches
in days gone by.   Now the death-day
had come to be   of the great battle-king,
when the Weder prince   met a wondrous end.
First they saw   a strange marvel there,
the loathsome serpent   lying on the ground
facing them.   The fire-dragon was burnt,
flame-scorched, cruel   and terrible in colour.
It was fifty   foot-lengths long
there as it lay.   Before, it had left
to lord it in the air   at night, to swoop low
and seek out its den.   Now, stilled in death,
it had come to the end   of its use of earth-caves.
Beside it goblets   and beakers were standing;
plates lay there   and precious swords,
eaten with rust,   as if in earth's hold
they had waited   a thousand winters.
That inheritance of old,   gold of the ancients,
was wound about   with a spell's bewitchment

so strong, that none   might stray inside
the hall of the hoard,   unless God himself,
true prince of victory   and protector of men,
let the wealth lie open   to one of his choosing,
and only the man   that he might think fit.

XLII

The hoard seems associated with occult powers of heathendom. A freeing
from its malign influence is needed for the poem's end to be achieved.

It was plain   the path had not prospered   3058–3136
for the creature that wrongly   kept hidden the wealth
at the wall. The warden   had laid waste a man
foremost among men;   but fully avenged
was its murderous deed.   A mystery it is
where and when a man   of brave fame may meet
his span's fated end,   to spend time no more
at home with his kinsmen   in the mead-hall.
So it was with Beowulf.   Till he sought out the sentinel
in the dark art of war,   he was unaware
of his way of world-parting,   by what it would be.
The high chieftains   who had hidden the hoard
had delivered a curse   till Doomsday upon it:
that the man who plundered   the place was a sinner
to be harshly punished,   imprisoned in unholy
devil-temples,   tight in hell's bonds.
But it was not so   with the one who went there
not blindly led   by a lust for gold.
    Wiglaf spoke,   son of Weohstan:
"Many must often   meet with distress,
as we do now,   when one has his way.
We could not persuade   our dear prince,
the land's protector,   of a prudent path,

not to go near   the guardian of gold,
but to let it lie   where it had lived long,
to keep its abode   till the end of the world.
He held to his high fate.   The hoard can be seen
that was hideously won;   the decree was too harsh
that drove him on,   the defender of the land.
I was inside   and saw it all,
the hall's great store,   when the chance was given;
but not as a friend   did I find my way in
below the earth-wall.   At once with my hands
I gathered up   a great and wonderful
heap of hoard-treasures   and carried them here
to my king and leader.   He was still living,
clear in his mind,   and much did he say
in his suffering. The old one   bid me salute you,
and said you must build,   to remember his deeds,
a high barrow   where the pyre burns,
one proud and tall.   In truth he was
the worthiest warrior   on the wide earth,
while he could still   have joy of his homestead.
Let us now go   that way again;
soon I shall take you   to see from up close
the wondrous heap   of jewelled work
at the wall's foot.   You will see well enough
the rings, the thick gold.   When we return
let the bier be made ready,   all rightly prepared;
and then let us carry   our lord and leader,
the beloved man   to where he shall long
know the protection   of the All-Powerful."
    Weohstan's son,   the heroic warrior,
issued an order   for wide announcement:
for men of property   and men in power
to provide wood for the fire   from far around
for the great one. He said,   "Let the dark flame grow,

the fire consume   the warrior king,
who often endured   a shower of iron,
when a storm of arrows,   unleashed by the string,
shot over the shield-wall,   each shaft driving on,
swift with the feather-flight   following the tip."
   Then did the wise   son of Weohstan
summon from the troop   seven together
of the king's retainers.   He called up the best
of the warriors, and with them   he went, making eight
under the evil roof.   One raised up
the light of fire   and went in front.
To loot the hoard needed   no drawing of lots;
as soon as the men   saw anything of it
lying unguarded   and going to waste
inside the cave,   there was little complaint,
as they rushed at once   to carry away
the wondrous treasure.   Over the cliff-wall
they heaved the dragon,   let the waves draw
the ornament-keeper   to the flood's arms.
The worked gold was loaded   onto a wagon,
an uncountable mass;   and the prince was carried,
the grey-haired warrior,   to Hronesness.

XLIII

An underlying pattern of movement to the funeral obsequies brings them
near, even as all is taken away.

The Géat people   got ready for him   3137–3182
a pyre on the ground   in no poor fashion:
it was hung with helmets   as he had asked,
shining breastplates,   shields of battle.
The lamenting nobles   laid in the midst
their famous leader   and beloved lord.

Then on the mound   the mightiest of pyres
was kindled by warriors;   the wood-smoke climbed
black over the blaze.   The burning roar mingled
with the noise of weeping –   the wind fell away –
till the fire had broken   to pieces the bone-house,
hot at the heart.   Heavily they spoke
of their deep sadness,   their liege lord's death.
A Géat woman   then began
a mourning lay;   with hair looped up,
she sang of her grief.   Ever and again
she uttered a fear   of days full of sorrow,
a heap of slaughter,   the terror of the host,
captivity, shame.   Heaven swallowed the smoke.
The Weder people   set to work building
a barrow on the headland;   it was high and broad,
to be seen by seafarers   far on the wave.
In ten days they made it,   the monument
to one brave in battle.   The burnt ashes
were walled about   most worthily,
in the finest way   that skilled men could fashion.
To the barrow they entrusted   the treasure and jewels,
all the ornaments   that earlier the men
with warlike heart   had taken from the hoard.
So they gave up   the gold to the ground,
the riches of old,   where it rests still,
of no use to men,   as of none before.
Twelve then rode   about the barrow,
sons of nobles,   strong in battle,
in deep lament   to mourn their king
and speak of him   in a lay of sorrow;
they told of his valour,   his noble virtue,
his glorious deeds.   So it is good
for a man to praise   his dear prince
and love him at heart,   when he must leave,

from the body's cover   be fetched away.
So they grieved,   the Géat people,
followers at hearth-fire,   their lord's fall.
They said he was,   among world-kings,
of men the mildest   and most gentle,
most gracious to his own,   most hopeful of honour.

THE DANISH ROYAL HOUSE (SCYLDINGS)

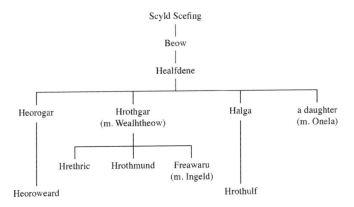

THE GÉAT ROYAL HOUSE (WEDERS)

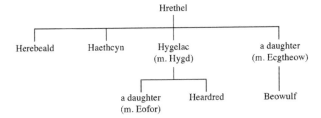

THE SWEDISH ROYAL HOUSE (SCYLFINGS)

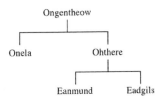